Virtual
Dating

Your Guide to a Relationship in a
SOCIALLY DISTANCED WORLD

Aleeza Ben Shalom
Author of *Get Real Get Married*

Marriage Minded Mentor LLC
coach@marriagemindedmentor.com
www.MarriageMindedMentor.com

Printed in the United States of America

First Edition

ISBN 9781975852955
EAN 9781975852955

Typesetting and Cover Design by: Joanna Dion Brown

Editing by: Alisa Roberts

Table of Contents

Praise for Virtual Dating
& Aleeza Ben Shalom

"*Virtual Dating exposed me to the possibility of finding love in an unconventional way, and provided me with the tools I needed to deal with the challenges that arose once I was in a cross-border/long distance relationship.*

Aleeza's guidance and tools have made virtual dating not only possible, but successful!"

– Sam C

"*Relevant and timely with the perfect dash of humor, Virtual Dating bridges the gap between what I know I should be doing with the information I need to actually do it by providing tips and tools on everything virtual dating related, from who should try it and why, to when to try it and how. I wasn't super confident in online dating before, but I certainly am now!*"

– Stephanie K

"*This step-by-step guide is geared specifically to the new realities we're facing and helped me on my dating journey move closer to finding THE ONE. "Virtual Dating" has me convinced that my soulmate is out there and that I now have the methods to find him, even in this time of social distancing.*"

– Shoshi G

Also Published by
Aleeza Ben Shalom
& Marriage Minded Mentor, LLC

Get Real Get Married
by Aleeza Ben Shalom

Point of Connection
by Leah Cheirif

Introduction

"Do I believe in computer dating? Only if the computers really love each other."

– Groucho Marx

I've been married for nearly 18 years. Back when I was single, online dating was just starting to come onto the scene, but was not yet the "in" thing. Today, as a dating and relationship coach, I help my clients attract quality dates, get over their dating hurdles and down the aisle. And in a world gone virtual, that means I'm guiding them through the process of online dating—and all the challenges that come with it.

We live in a world that's gone virtual. Think about what your daily routine looks like: alarm clock rings to the tune of your favorite song; morning meditation on the Headspace app; checking social media and the news; reviewing your schedule for the day; office meetings via Zoom; fantasy football and Netflix downtime...you get the idea.

If all of that already makes up a significant portion of our daily programming, why would dating be different?

Despite what your grandparents might tell you, you can develop a healthy relationship—with the potential to lead to marriage—online. You can, in fact, find your soulmate with an online search, the swipe of a finger and some fast-paced thumb clicking.

But you have to know how, or online dating will likely be everything your grandparents make it out to be: short-lived and pointless.

My goal in writing Virtual Dating is to provide you with a relationship roadmap that will help you progress your relationship from a virtual "I like you" to an in-person "I want to marry you." The chapters in this book outline a step-by-step process for accomplishing just that, as well as best practices to follow throughout the process, and a how-to for making the transition from virtual dating to in-person dating.

But before you continue reading, I will say this: virtual dating is not for everyone.

I do believe that connecting with your soulmate and developing a relationship online is absolutely possible, and this relationship roadmap will work for many people. However, if you are the type of person who simply hates the online stuff and you don't believe that there's any way you could make this work, then don't.

This doesn't mean there's anything wrong with you or that you need to try until you make it work! There isn't, and you don't. The sooner you acknowledge and get comfortable with that reality, the quicker you can move on to pursuing an in-person relationship right off the bat without wasting anyone's time online. So if you fall into that category, I recommend that you close this book, gift wrap it, and send it to a friend who would appreciate it. Try my first book, *Get Real, Get Married,* if you'd like some practical advice and strategies for in-person dating.

If you're still reading, I trust you are ready for this. You're marriage-minded, your mind is open to this process, and you have a belief that this is a form of dating that could work for you. Great! But before we dive in, there are three things I want you to keep in mind.

1. You need to be in a healthy place for an online relationship.

Make sure you are ready for this, physically, mentally and emotionally, the same way you would when starting a relationship in person. If you would say no to an in-person date because you've got some stuff you need to work through first, don't say yes to an online date. You still need to work through that same stuff first.

If you're in a negative headspace and believe this could never work, then I'd suggest you stop dating for the time being. It isn't fair to either of you if you dive into a virtual relationship thinking that it isn't as "real" or as serious as an in-person one.

You can, instead, use this time as an opportunity to take a dating detox. Spend some time doing some inner work and figuring out what's holding you back. If there's something specific you know you need to work on before you'll be ready for a relationship, focus on that. At the same time, reflect on your dating history. Assess what has worked and what hasn't, and come up with a plan of action for once you feel ready to date.

2. There are times to avoid virtual dating.

Well, more specifically, there are times to avoid beginning an online relationship.

The first is around holiday times. The two weeks before and after any major holiday can be particularly difficult to start something new because there's so much happening in the world around you. I affectionately call the time surrounding holidays "Temporary Insanity" because people often make weird dating decisions during this time.

The prospect of seeing family and friends at an upcoming holiday often compels some people to make sure to have somebody by their side. Or to have a story about their latest date or relationship.

This motivation does not lend itself to long-term relationships.

Additionally, meeting someone before a holiday will cause a break in the dating momentum, which is not an ideal way to start a relationship. Therefore, it's best to avoid starting anything for two weeks before or after any major holiday.

The second time to avoid starting something new is when you're evading loneliness. One of the greatest challenges that single men and women face is loneliness. As social beings, we were designed to interact with others on a regular basis. This is true whether you are an extrovert or introvert. As a result, when you're feeling lonely, spending time with others often fills a void. However, while it may be effective, seeking a date is not a healthy way to fill that social void.

I'd much rather you rely on friends and family to give you an emotional lift. Go into the date with a feeling of wholesomeness, of looking to add something valuable to your life, rather than looking to fill empty space. Do not depend on your date to make you feel better or less bored.

Being needy is not attractive and is often a red flag when starting a relationship. So if you're feeling lonely, take some time to connect with friends and family. Do your best to remove that ache, and then enter a relationship healthy, grounded and in a place where you are able to connect with someone for positive reasons.

3. The content in this book is ageless.

I've worked with clients as young as 18 and as old as 89 (not kidding!), and interestingly enough, despite the seventy-one-year difference, the coaching that I do remains quite similar. The foundation for developing a good relationship doesn't change with the passing of years.

So whether you're 23, 43 or 73, know that whatever you're reading in this book is relevant to you. Obviously, the specifics of your situation are different than the next person's, but the relationship roadmap outlined here remains the same regardless of your age.

Though we've already established virtual dating as an option for you, I'm sure you've still got lots of questions. Here are a few I hear often:

- *How will we truly develop a relationship when we can't even grab a cup of coffee together?*
- *Can we sustain a new, virtual relationship over a long period of time? Won't things get stale if we can't switch up our dating location and activities?*
- *How can we date if we can't touch?*
- *When we do finally meet, how will we transition from a virtual relationship to an in-person one?*

I put these questions here because I want to let you know that you won't finish this book without having the answers. I highly recommend reading each chapter in order, but if there's a question that you simply must know the answer to, feel free to browse the table of contents. You'll probably find the chapter that will provide you with the information you're seeking.

Takeaway: Virtual dating is an option for anyone who is open to the process, in a healthy place and ready for a relationship.

Exercise: Virtual Dating Thoughts

Now that we've set the stage, we're just about ready to open the curtain!

But before we do, I'd like you to complete the following self-evaluation. There are exercises at the end of every chapter, and I believe that doing them will help you get the most out of this book. So grab a pen!

Step 1: Rate your feelings

On a scale of 1 to 10, how do you feel about virtual dating as of this moment? (1 = Meh, I never really liked the idea of it and I'm pretty skeptical that it could actually work for me; 10 = I think it's the most awesome way to date and am confident I can find my soulmate through virtual dating).

— 1 — 2 — 3 — 4 — 5 — 6 — 7 — 8 — 9 — 10 —

Step 2: Write your thoughts

Jot down any thoughts and feelings you have about virtual dating. (Remember, there's no right or wrong answer here, so just listen to your gut and get it all out.)

_____

_____

_____

_____

_____

_____

_____

_____

_____

_____

_____

_____

_____

_____

_____

Chapter One:
Waze To Date

"Distance does to love what wind does to fire, extinguishes the weak and fuels the strong."
– Roger De Bussy-Rabutin

How long have you been navigating the world of virtual dating?

Online dating has been around since the invention of video chatting. AOL, Skype, Google Hangouts and the like have been helping couples in long-distance relationships for years. However, back in the day (and by that I mean in 2019), we didn't call long-distance dating virtual dating. Long-distance relationships weren't virtual; they were just...not in person as often.

The year 2020 took virtual dating from a less desirable or a "just for fun" option to the dating method of choice. In fact, for the vast majority of the world, it was the only way to date because of the COVID-19 pandemic. As a result, over the last six months, I've been working almost exclusively with clients who are dating virtually. And while COVID-19 may have been just a passing (though impactful) season in our lifetime, it has significantly changed how we date.

Over the last several months, when there were no social gatherings, religious occasions or work events, tens of thousands more singles began dating online. Virtual relationships have become the norm. And as singles were forced to navigate those relationships, digital dating took on more meaning than it used to have. It became something more meaningful and significant. Singles worldwide are more open to virtual relationships, to taking them seriously and giving them time to develop—even when they can't meet anytime soon.

I've spoken to many singles who are so happy about the results they are getting through online speed dating events or virtual gatherings. Some have even told me they have met more potential prospects in the eight weeks of being online than in the two years of in-person dating they'd done prior to that! Many of my clients have been developing and maintaining new relationships that started online.

I've spoken to many singles who are so happy about the results they are getting through online speed dating events or virtual gatherings.

In this book, I have combined my experiences helping clients through old-school online dating with guiding clients through this new age of virtual dating. All that experience has added up to create the perfect guide for you.

> Joe and Rachel[1] met on Zoom.
>
> They were two of sixty singles taking part in a virtual dating experiment: a Zoom mixer.
>
> They went from interacting with the entire group to a smaller breakout room and then, upon request, to their own private meeting.
>
> It was going well. Very well. But then Joe wondered outloud if the meeting would end when they reached their free Zoom meeting time limit. They had to quickly decide how to continue before reaching that limit.
>
> Rachel said, "My number is 610-555-4906..." The screen went blank.

You know that virtual dating is popular by default right now. But I want to share my top three benefits of virtual dating.

---

[1] Names have been changed for confidentiality.

Benefit 1: *Expanding your search might be the missing piece to finding your soulmate.*

Imagine the dating site you're on matches you with somebody who lives far away. In the past, you would have never considered chatting with this person because of the distance. You've always been focused on getting to date in person, so it was simply a non-starter.

But now, you are more open to dating someone long-distance, and so you begin to chat. You start with messages through the dating site you met on, then move to video chats. You video frequently. You like each other. I mean, you really like each other. You continue to develop a meaningful connection and eventually decide to take this to the next level by meeting in person. So you do. And you realize you were truly destined for each other. You get engaged, then married—and before you know it, you're walking off into the sunset together.

Okay, so that was a sped-up version of reality, but you see my point.

Maybe your dating profile needs updating, or maybe you need some text coaching (read on for both!). But you may have come up empty on your search simply because your soulmate lives in another city. Or because they recently moved overseas. Or because they're in the military and never in one place for long. Expanding your search beyond your local limits might be the one action that provides you the opportunity to meet the person you were destined to meet.

Benefit 2: *You have to take things slowly.*

Yes, this is a benefit.

Taking things slowly gives you more room for processing. It allows you to focus on work and your personal life while also developing a relationship. This allows for a much healthier balance in your life.

It also takes off some pressure to progress the relationship too quickly. I have a saying I tell my clients all the time: "You can only move as fast as the slowest person in the relationship."

It's rare to have two completely unique individuals in a relationship who are on exactly the same page every step of the way. It's common for one to be ready to move forward sooner than the other.

Virtual dating actually works to the benefit of both individuals in this case.

If you're the slower one, this process gives you space to figure things out and move forward at a leisurely pace. Because of the nature of an online relationship, it'll take more time to develop than if you were in person, allowing you to get to know the other person without feeling like you're rushing into things.

"You can only move as fast as the slowest person in the relationship."

If you're the quicker one, this process automatically slows things down for you (as mentioned above). Since you aren't moving too fast, you have a better chance of things not fizzling out as quickly as they showed up (think: fireworks and sparklers versus a romantic candle). And it comes with the added bonus of feeling less impatience toward the person you're dating.

Benefit 3: *You won't be able to touch.*

Yes, again, this is a benefit.

As a general rule, I recommend you hold off on touching, especially at the beginning of a relationship. I recommend this for in-person relationships too! While this can definitely be challenging at times, it effectively allows you to decide whether you actually like the human being in front of you without being distracted by the physical connection.

Many faith-based cultures have rules surrounding physical intimacy between dating couples prior to marriage as a show of the spiritual power that intimacy embodies. This abstinence actually sets the foundation for an enhanced physical, mental, emotional and spiritual experience once they do finally touch. Although this may not be your custom, it has worked for many couples over the course of thousands of years, and I strongly suggest you give it a try.

Virtual dating takes the challenge out of not touching. Here, there is simply no choice.

Oh, and Joe and Rachel? He did call her. Their recent wedding had exactly 10 people present, all masked and socially distanced. And it was amazing.

Takeaway: Virtual dating is not just a default dating approach, but one that comes with its own benefits. You can find your soulmate and life partner by dating online.

Exercise: Make Some Space

Move an app on your phone that you use often to a new space on your homescreen. Your brain is used to it being in a certain place, and you will have to learn to adjust to the new space it's in. Most likely you'll be irritated at the beginning as your fingers will automatically jump to its old spot and it won't be there. After a week your brain will begin to develop new neural pathways and will start to remember where the app is and you won't be as frustrated with the new location.

The goal of this exercise is to ready your brain for the new changes that are coming your way with your new relationship. It's a conscious reminder that bringing someone into your life will rearrange things, and you have to make mental space and move things around to allow someone to come into your life and remain there permanently. Start to make space in your life for your person even when you haven't found them yet.

Chapter Two:
Online Overhaul

"Online dating versus traditional dating is like using an electronic calculator versus an abacus. They both give you accurate results if used properly, but one of them is obviously faster and easier in the modern age."
–Newton Lee

Now that we've covered the benefits, I'm sure you're ready to dive in. You're ready to learn the how-tos, best practices and dos-and-don'ts of virtual dating. That's good. The more you know, the more prepared you are, and the more likely you are to find your soulmate online. But before we talk about the practical application of digital dates, I want to help you get yourself set up for attracting quality dates.

Tell me what you would prefer: lots and lots of matches but no one you're excited about, or a more select group made up entirely of the kind of life partner you're actually looking for?

With so many people dating online, it can be easy to get caught up in choosing the most open settings on your dating profile and just swiping right. And it can be equally easy to get lost in the sea of singles.

I believe that the best way to make this process as painless and productive as possible is by making sure that the way you are seen online reflects the way you want to be seen, so that you are attracting the right kind of person to you.

Think about how much simpler online dating would be if you didn't have to wade through the non-starters, and instead got to pick from a handful of quality options. That is the goal of this chapter.

What's the first thing you do when you are matched with a prospective date?

We're in the 21st century. Of course the answer is "Google them!"

You're going to check them out. You're going to try to get as much information as you can possibly get from the web. Why? Well, because it's available and you want to know if this could be a good match.

That means that anyone who got matched with you is doing the exact same thing.

They're Googling you. And what I want to know is this: do you know what they're seeing?

I mean, sure, you know you have a public Instagram account, that you've deleted all those wild college party pictures from Facebook, and there's that one article writeup from the time you won a year's worth of free ice cream from your local ice cream shop for submitting the winning name "Today's Sundae."

But do you know what else is floating around in cyberspace that you aren't even aware of? Did you know that picture of your middle school MMA competition where you were totally knocked out is still up on their extra-curriculars page? Or that you are named as the person with the highest number of Coca-Cola shares bought at the cheapest price?

Maybe you care about some things, maybe you don't. Maybe you can edit some things, maybe you can't. Either way, it's important that you know what exists.

"Well, if I can't change it, why is it important?" I'm so glad you asked.

First, because there's a decent chance that your date will bring up something they found online in conversation, and you don't want to be thrown off guard. If you know what information exists about you online, then you won't be surprised when someone else mentions that they saw it.

Hopefully, they won't be like my client Miri's date, who had gone through every single one of her public Facebook posts and then quoted her comment responses back to her. But even if they are...at least you'll know where it came from.

Second, it's possible that there's stuff out there about you that does not properly portray the image of how you want others to see you. We all go through a series of ups, downs and sideways during our lives, and there may be some content out there that you believe just doesn't represent who you are now.

By knowing what's out there, you have an opportunity to give your online presence an overhaul and ensure that what others see when they Google you represents you—and the vision you want them to have of you.

Lastly, nowadays, if there isn't much that comes up when someone Googles you, that can be a red flag. If someone matches with you and then can't find any information about you, like not even a LinkedIn profile or any social media mention, they're going to wonder what's up with that.

So even if you are a very private person (which is totally okay, and I have clients like that), I would encourage you to consider intentionally putting up some information about yourself. It doesn't have to be extremely personal, but enough to indicate that you're not a secret assassin or a catfisher.

In this case, I would also recommend Googling your family members to see what comes up for them. If somebody can't find enough information on you, they're going to look around to see what pieces they can gather to put together the puzzle of who you are.

As I was coaching my client Dan through the Online Overhaul process, he came to me with a predicament. A number of years ago, a close family member of his had been charged with a white-collar crime, and that information was public and still easily accessible. So accessible in fact, that when anyone Googled Dan's family name, a report of the incident popped up in the first three Google results.

Not exactly the kind of thing anyone wants a potential date seeing, especially before they've gotten to know each other.

Dan and I spent some time discussing this and ultimately came to the conclusion that there was really nothing he could do about the situation. There was no way to get that report taken off the web, and there was no way he could avoid having his name Googled.

So instead of stressing about that, we focused on coming up with a neutral explanation that he could share with potential dates whenever it did come up. We spoke about the relationship Dan has with this family member, how this incident affected him personally and what his date does or doesn't need to know about it. This way, he was not thrown off guard in the moment; he did not come across as defensive, nor did he refute the fact that the crime had occurred.

By doing this preparation, Dan set himself up for success. He was confident in his response, rather than constantly wondering whether and when someone would bring it up, which in turn allowed him to be more present and focused on the actual date.

Alright, so you Googled yourself. Now what?

First, gather all the information about yourself that exists online today. I want you to list up to 10 different places where your name comes up in a search, note what kind of information is there (write ups, profiles, images, reviews, work-related, personal etc.) and whether it's positive, negative or neutral. You can use the worksheet at the end of this chapter.

Keep in mind when looking at that information that something you think is positive might actually be neutral. Or something you think is negative might not be for somebody else. This is your personal judgment of that information, so do your best to view it from an objective perspective. Obviously, that's easier said than done, so if you're struggling with this exercise, ask a friend for some help.

Next, identify what you want to change and what is actually within your control to change. Make a list of what you'd like to edit and/or delete.

For example, you might want to change things that are on your social media feed. Maybe you have photos and posts of you from ten years ago that you're a little bit uncomfortable with today. Maybe you look or sound different, or maybe that image of yourself doesn't reflect who you are now. If it doesn't sit right with you today, then don't present it to the world.

Aim for only having stuff out there that you're okay with right now. Just because you once posted it doesn't mean it has to remain online. You can easily delete content or change a privacy setting so that only close friends—or only you—can see it.

And then don't focus on the things that you can't change (but again, it's good to know what's there). Dan's case is an example of something that he probably can't change. Most of us don't have the ability to edit old newspaper archives or official government content.

With that said, if there is something that exists online that bothers you enough, you can always reach out to the newspaper or your local office and say, "Hey, the following content (provide a link) no longer represents who I am, and I'm wondering if you can please take that down?" Most likely, it won't happen; but you never know, and it's definitely worth a shot. Just don't spend too much time on those pieces of information and don't stress about them too much. Focus on what's within your control.

Remember that the information itself will not stop your soulmate from choosing you. It might be a little hurdle that you have to get over, but there are lots of hurdles that people have to get over in relationships. Accept that this is one of your things.

I would suggest having some prepared responses you can share in the event that your date does bring up this information.

Also, don't forget about page two of Google. I've had clients who were doing an online overhaul who have said to me, "Aleeza, I really hope nobody gets to page two." But here's the thing: there's a 50-50 chance that they will. So do yourself a favor, and check page two.

Once you've got your "to edit" list, it's time to prioritize which items you want to work with, and in what order. There is a worksheet at the end of the chapter where you can keep notes of what edits need to be made as well as any pertinent information you want to remember as you make those changes.

The best way to prioritize this list is by starting with what is easiest for you to deal with today and ending with the most challenging pieces. It's so much easier when you start with the easy stuff. It leaves you feeling accomplished, motivated, and ready for the next thing on your list.

As you complete each piece, simply check off the box so you know it's done.

I recommend that you do an online overhaul every six months to a year, because information surfaces on a regular basis. So make a note in your calendar on a date six months away, and Google yourself again then. Go through the same process of making a list, checking it twice, and working your way through any changes from easiest to hardest.

If you find that there's nothing on that list in six months from now that needs to be edited, great! There doesn't have to be. But it's always worth the check.

Takeaway: Make sure that your online persona reflects the true you so that you attract the kind of person that you're looking for.

Exercise: Online Overhaul

Step 1: Gather all your online information.

LOCATION	CONTENT TYPE	POS/NEG/NEUT + NOTES
1._____	_____	_____
2._____	_____	_____
3._____	_____	_____
4._____	_____	_____
5._____	_____	_____
6._____	_____	_____
7._____	_____	_____
8._____	_____	_____
9._____	_____	_____
10._____	_____	_____

Step 2: Make a list of what information you'd like to edit and/or delete.

LOCATION	EDIT/DELETE/NOTES	
1._____	_____	☐
2._____	_____	☐
3._____	_____	☐

4._____ _____ ☐

5._____ _____ ☐

6._____ _____ ☐

7._____ _____ ☐

8._____ _____ ☐

9._____ _____ ☐

10. _____ _____ ☐

Chapter Three:
Hooked on You

"Fair warning, I'm a wimp when it comes to spicy foods."
– David G, Marriage Minded Mentor client

One 4th of July a local chef and his sous chef, along with a small-town news network, took over a client's kitchen. The premise? They had six hours to prepare a gourmet BBQ—with whatever she already had in her kitchen.

The sous chef began pulling random things from the cabinets and fridge. Sardines, spaghetti sauce, apple puree, nectarines, eggs, sauerkraut, cumin, chia seeds and fresh garlic. They piled about fifty different food items on the counter, took a step back to assess, and then began working through it.

The chef then picked out the items to work with and put them to the side. He put back anything that didn't fit with the recipe he was developing in his mind. He wavered over a couple additional spices, but in the end decided they wouldn't enhance the dish much, and instead chose to highlight a few spices that would really pop. Then they got to work.

That year's BBQ? It was the best they'd ever had!

Your dating bio is your online first impression. And the truth is, like my client in the story above, you've already got all you need to make that first impression amazing. You might just need a little help choosing what to highlight to make you sound divine.

In my ten years as a dating coach, I have read through thousands of dating profiles. When I see a profile that has all of the traditional information, stated in a way that could describe any man or any woman, it leaves me cold.

I have no idea who you really are or what you're looking for...and you're not memorable.

The thing is, I want to remember you. I want YOU to stand out.

I'm looking for something that is unique or different about you. Something that can't be used to describe hundreds or thousands of other people. Or, at the very least, I want the way you describe that something to be unique and memorable.

Whether you've got space for two lines on a dating app or two paragraphs on an online profile, your first sentence is what will draw attention. That first line is what will attract the right person and ensure that they stick around to continue reading the rest of your profile. Or—equally valuable!—it will repel the wrong person.

Every good book starts with a hook. There's something that draws you in and compels you to read more. Usually it's right at the beginning of the story. Are you going to continue reading after the first page if you do not like what you see? Probably not.

Your profile is a super-abridged version of the book of you.

Nobody is going to continue reading your entire profile if they don't like the first line. So we've got to grab them! You want to pull them in and essentially say, "Look at me, check out my profile."

And if the person reading your profile is totally not for you, you want them to take one look at your hook and then move right along on their merry way.

So how do you create a hook?

Go through your existing profiles and gather all the information that you have written down about yourself. Then sift through the content, think about what goes together well, decide what you're going to keep and what you're going to get rid of, and make decisions about what else you might need in order to build this gourmet hook.

Here's one client's hook: "If there was a snowstorm and I had to be stuck in one store, it'd be a tough call between Michaels Arts and Crafts and Barnes and Noble."

This is one simple line that not only catches my attention, but gives me a feel for the person who wrote it. She likes crafts, she likes reading, she has a sense of humor. It's charming—and for the right person, captivating. If I'm also a bibliophile or crafter then I'm already excited to read more.

I'm going to look through her profile because it grabbed my attention and roped me in. I want to know more about this person. She got me. Hook, line and sinker.

But not every hook has to be captivating. It just can't be boring.

I told one client that we needed to find him a hook. His response was, "Nah, I don't have one." I told him that if I looked through his five-paragraph dating profile, I'd find his hook. And, as predicted, about three quarters of the way through the page I see, "Fair warning, I'm a wimp when it comes to spicy food."

I excitedly proclaimed, "That's your hook!" He was totally confused because, "It doesn't tell you anything about me."

"It doesn't have to," I explained. "A hook just has to draw the reader in. It can simply share a random piece of information...as long as it's interesting."

Your hook doesn't have to explicitly state something that you would typically use to define yourself. Likely, those things are the same things that lots of other people use to define themselves. You want something different. You want something that shares insight without being obvious about it.

Your hook should include a piece of random or intriguing information. It can be light, it can be playful, it can be intense, it can be funny, it can be something that puts a smile on your reader's face, it can be something that makes them pause and think twice. Usually, it's something that'll make someone else say, "Hmm, I want to know more about this person."

In this client's case, even if I like spicy food, I'm probably still going to read the profile. I'm not turned off by the fact that he doesn't like spicy food. In fact, I'm impressed that he owns it and uses it as a way to share some humor while implying that while he might be a wimp when it comes to spicy foods, he's not a wimp when it comes to other things.

Here are some more samples to get your mind stimulated and thinking so you get an idea of what a hook sounds like. I hope that you will find inspiration here to help you with yours.

"I'm easy going until you get to know me."

"I dance a fine line between complexity and awesomeness."

"I'm a person who sees the world in shades of gray rather than black and white."

In the last example, you might draw in that person who sees those shades of gray with you, or you might attract that person who does see black and white but appreciates somebody else who can see shades of gray to complement them.

Or how about this one?

"My first memory as a child is a magician putting flour, and eggs, and milk into a pot, and pulling out a white rabbit."

This tells me absolutely nothing about this person's personality. Instead, it gives me a cute memory, a visual of an impressionable moment that makes me wonder what else they're willing to share in this profile, along with the unexpressed understanding that they seek magical moments in their life.

Now it's time to find yours.

Takeaway: Create an intriguing one liner that'll attract the attention of the right person and invite them to learn more.

Exercise: Create Your Hook

Step 1: Write...

Start by compiling any and all dating profiles you currently have, on- or offline. If you don't have any, no worries; now's the perfect time to create one. Looking at the information that you have, notice any particular details that jump out at you as being different, unique or make you think "that's so me."

If you find such a detail, that can probably be edited into your hook. If you don't, you can definitely develop one from scratch.

If you're creative and writing comes naturally to you, this will probably be a fairly easy process. If you're not, don't get overwhelmed. Give yourself time to find the perfect hook, and feel free to recruit a friend who's got some creative writing skills.

Sometimes a hook takes a couple of days to craft and sometimes it takes a week or more.

Here are some hook starters that you can play with to help you find your own.

My personal philosophy is...
I grew up on...
Lately I have been...

I fill my days / nights with...
I'm in tune with...
I believe...
I'm passionate about...
My dream is...
What I love about my work...
I'm drawn to...

Come up with 2 to 3 hook ideas that you really like and write them down here.

1._____

_____

2._____

_____

3._____

_____

Step 2: ...and share!

Share the hooks above with your family and friends and gather feedback. Pick your favorite one to use on your dating profile and update it ASAP.

Chapter Four:
Soulmate Summary

*"I'm looking for someone who would dance in the rain alone if she
thought it was fun, rather than a cookie-cutter gal."*
- Josh H, Marriage Minded Mentor client

"What are you looking for?" It's the most common—and most dreaded—
question that singles get. They get asked this question from well-meaning
friends, family, and yes, even strangers. And while it is (usually) asked
from a place of thoughtfulness, many individuals are still sick and tired of
the question! When I asked my clients why that was the case, there were
two common responses that came up over and over again.

First, they feel like oftentimes people ask because they're "supposed
to." Sometimes it really is about you—they believe you want to be considered and asked. And sometimes it's actually about them—they feel like
they're doing their part in helping you find your soulmate simply by asking. The fact that there often isn't any follow-up is what has led so many
singles to come to detest this question.

Second, and often as a result of the previous reason, many singles
don't believe that the listener will actually do anything with the information they share. They don't even have high hopes that they will be
understood.

So, often, they just let a whole bunch of words fall out of their mouths.
Sometimes it does reflect what they're looking for; but more often than

not, it's a jumble of points that don't paint a clear picture of the kind of person they're seeking.

Does any of this sound familiar to you?

I'm going to offer a different perspective I'd like you to consider. You can take as much time as you need to process what I'm about to tell you, but know that I believe in it 100%.

Every person that you encounter, every person who asks you "So what are you looking for?" is a potential matchmaker.

When you have a well-articulated answer to that question, and can succinctly describe what you're looking for in a life partner, the person you're talking to can potentially help you. They can now keep you in mind and actually make a suggestion when they come across an individual that fits that picture.

That well-articulated, succinct answer is what I call your "Soulmate Summary."

I've found that many singles answer the so-what-are-you-looking-for question based on whether or not they believe the questioner can help. Which means that different people get different replies. Like, you probably don't give the same response to your grandma as you do to your elementary school teacher you bumped into at the pizza shop. Or the same one to a friend who's known you for years versus a venture capitalist you met at a fundraising event last week.

The problem with this is that you never know who might be the messenger that actually knows your soulmate and can send them your way. If you considered for a moment that every one of those people I mentioned might be the one who'll connect you with "the one," you'd probably give them all the same response, right? Because it does actually matter that they have this important bit of information if they're going to play a role in setting you up.

And that's where the Soulmate Summary comes in.

By having a few sentences right at the tip of your tongue that express exactly the kind of person you're seeking, without you having to stop and think it over, you take pressure off of yourself. You don't have to think of a response every time, and you stop having to consider whether or not it's worth sharing your thoughts.

I don't want you to judge whether or not a specific person will or won't help you. If somebody comes into your life and they're asking, I'm asking you to assume that they're being genuine and sincere and they really do want to help you. And you should give them a real answer—because with a real answer, they have the best opportunity to try to set you up with the right person. They simply can't begin to try without the right kind of information.

Not only that, but when they find themselves at the receiving end of a well-thought-out response that you've clearly put time and consideration into composing, they realize that you're serious. And if you're serious, it inspires them to be serious too. Other people feed off of your energy, so when you show up and express that you're ready to find your soulmate, they will believe that and will want to help in any way they can.

I believe that part of the reason that so many people ask and then don't actually do anything or follow up (a pet peeve of singles as discussed above), is because so often singles unintentionally give off a vibe that says, "I don't believe that you can help me, so stop wasting my time." I know, that seems a little extreme, and you would never say anything like this. But haven't you ever felt this way? If you felt it, I'm pretty sure that they did too!

Another reason they may not have set you up yet is that they actually did pay attention to what you're looking for...and haven't met that person yet. This is like a seed that is planted but hasn't sprouted yet. It could be they will make a suggestion when they meet someone appropriate for you.

So don't give up on your potential matchmakers so fast.

Now here's the deal when it comes to virtual dating.

Although everything I just shared was from the perspective of in-person interactions, the reality is that you'll still get asked this question online. Whether it's within a social media group for marriage-minded singles or on a dating site that has live matchmakers, this is a question you're going to come across. Even your online dating profile will probably ask you for this information.

Additionally, think about all your friends who are also dating virtually. You might be seeing them, chatting about dating prospects, or comparing notes. One of them may actually have come across a potential prospect for you and they might be open to making an intro. So when they ask you what you're looking for, you're going to give them your Soulmate Summary too.

So take the time to work on this now. Make yourself that perfectly crafted three-liner that explains what you're looking for in a concise, clear, meaningful way that you feel confident sharing over and over and over again. You will actually save yourself energy further along in the process by doing this work now.

Takeaway: Be ready to confidently express what you're looking for without mumbling, stumbling or fumbling.

Exercise: Your Soulmate Summary

Step 1: Brainstorm

The first thing that you're going to do is actually write down the first things that come to mind when I ask "So, what are you looking for?"

Don't overthink it; just write down the top few responses that you normally share with people. You might find it helpful to say it out loud (you can even record yourself and then listen to the recording) and then copy that down. This information is going to give you the starting point for pulling your Soulmate Summary together.

_____

_____

_____

_____

_____

_____

_____

_____

_____

Step 2: Edit

Next you're going to look at the information you jotted down and make an accounting of the content here. Just like you did with your hook in the last chapter, you're going to assess what should stay and what should go. Which pieces of information do you actually like and feel are important? Which pieces are making you think, "Nah, I don't really want/need to say that?" And what other information got left out but really should be included here?

Just to be clear, everything you put down might be true about what you're looking for. It just might not be the most important information to include.

Want to Share: _____

_____

_____

Should Delete: _____

_____

_____

Currently Missing/Should Be Added: _____

_____

_____

Once you have an outline of content based on the previous two steps, it's time to pull it together.

Step 3: Practice

In terms of talk time, this should be short and sweet. Aim for approximately 30 seconds (one minute maximum). That translates into about three to seven sentences. This is not an essay that includes everything you could possibly want in a life partner. It's just enough information to give somebody a brief but clear idea of what you're looking for.

Keep in mind that you're going to be using your Soulmate Summary both online and offline. That means you will be verbally sharing this information with people you encounter on a regular basis, so keep the content conversation friendly. Don't use sophisticated language with complex grammar structure that will just sound awkward when chatting with your neighbor or when you meet an old friend at the grocery store.

When you feel comfortable with your final draft, read it out loud. If it sounds right, you're done! If you feel like something's wrong with it, go back and revise it. Reading it out loud might help you flesh it out.

This is a multi-step process, so don't get annoyed or frustrated with it. Patience is your friend here. Your Soulmate Summary should contain information that you're excited to share, in language that suits you and that flows easily, so take your time with it.

_____

_____

_____

_____

_____

_____

_____

Step 4: Share

There's a Jewish saying that says "a person will be led in the way that he desires to go." I think this means that the more you are clear about the kind of person you are looking for, the more likely you are to find him or her. And to make that even more practical, the more you share that information with those around you, the easier it will be for someone else to help you.

What I mean to say is, now that you've got your Soulmate Summary, share it! Share it online, share it with your friends and family, share it with the world. Put it out there, let people know you're ready and clear about the kind of person your soulmate is, and let the wheels start turning.

Chapter Five:
Navigating Networking

"Matchmaker, matchmaker, make me a match, find me a find, catch me a catch."
– "Matchmaker, Matchmaker,"
from Fiddler on the Roof, by Jerry Bock and Sheldon Harnick

Have you heard that overused quote, "Your network is your net worth"?

Well, I'm going to tell you right now that while I don't agree with that (because I believe you're so much more than your network), I do believe that the value of your network is what will determine your potential for opportunity. And that is true whether we're talking about business, friendships, or, in this case, soulmates.

Now, don't get me wrong. I'm not saying that if you're the kind of person who prefers an intimate, private group of friends over a giant social network, or you're just not a people person and have a hard time connecting with others, that you won't find your soulmate. Let me be clear: that's not what I'm saying at all.

What I am saying is that the more people you know, the more social reach you can create, the easier it is to utilize your network for meeting your Mr. or Mrs. Right. It's like fishing. If you have one fishing rod in the water, there's a chance you'll catch a fish. But if you put five different lines in the water, strategically placing them at appropriately distanced intervals, there's a much higher chance that you'll catch a great fish.

Now, obviously, the chances of you catching something aren't just dependent on how many fishing lines you're using; where you choose to go fishing, and the quality of bait you've hooked, will significantly impact your opportunity for catching the fish of your choice. (That last tortured analogy brings us back to your Hook and your Soulmate Summary. Good thing you've already got those covered!)

Where you choose to fish for your soulmate (online, offline, etc.), how many different fishing lines you choose to throw in (dating apps, matchmakers, online groups or meetups, etc.), and the kinds of fish you're baiting (making sure that the groups, sites and apps that you're on actually host the kind of person you're seeking) are all things to take into consideration. But keep in mind that whatever choices you make for where to fish, utilizing your network is going to expand your potential for opportunity. So let's make sure you have the maximum potential!

Social Media

The first thing to do is to connect online with all the people you know offline. The reason for this is simple. If you are Facebook friends with your barista, mechanic or orthodontist, they'll see your social media posts and you'll likely be on their minds a lot more than you would have been if you weren't connected via social networks.

If your experience is anything like mine, your favorite barista moved out of state last summer, your mechanic only gets a visit from you once every six months (at least you pray it isn't more than that) and you don't even use your orthodontist anymore! But again, if your experience is like mine, you'll still be connecting with those very people every few days by liking, commenting on and, once in a while, getting into a heated debate on each other's posts.

While obviously social media isn't an exact reflection of day-to-day life, it does still keep you connected and in each other's lives in a way that you might not be otherwise.

So I want you to make a list of all the people in your life that you aren't yet connected with online and follow or friend them on whatever platform is most appropriate. It could be Instagram, Facebook, LinkedIn, Twitter, TikTok, SnapChat, or anything that you're both actively engaged on.

I will add that, personally, I believe you're best off sticking to just one or two platforms that you interact on most regularly. If you're a Twitter guy and some of the people you know hang out on Facebook, it's not going to be very helpful if you make an account there in order to connect with them, but then you don't actually post or engage there. If you're a Twitter guy, stick to Twitter.

Don't worry if this process takes you some time, that's normal. Use the exercise at the end of this chapter to help you brainstorm.

Once you've got your list started—and keep in mind that you don't have to have it completed before doing this next bit—it's time to actually connect with them. Send a friend request. If for whatever reason your request isn't accepted, don't stress about it. Some people have personal boundaries around who they connect with online and it's not an indication of their feelings toward you. In those circumstances, just move on.

When you've officially connected, I would recommend that you reach out with a short personal message and/or comment on a recent post of theirs. This interaction is noted by the platform's algorithm and ensures that you now see more of each other. Which is exactly what we want.

If you feel comfortable, make it even more productive and send them your Hook and Soulmate Summary with a message like: "I'm happy we've connected online! I would like to share with you that I am currently actively and intentionally seeking my soulmate. I've attached a brief overview of what I'm looking for and hope that if you think of someone who you believe might be a good fit, you'll make an introduction. Would love to hear how things are with [insert personal comment here]."

If you don't feel comfortable doing that just yet, that's fine. Connect with a basic message and with time, as you interact more and more with each other online, I believe you'll get to a point where you feel okay sending that message.

Or they may see this information if you post it on your own page. Which brings me to my next suggestion. This was actually something that I noticed a client of mine doing.

Sara was not a fan of in-person singles events and, after multiple negative experiences, disliked working with matchmakers. That left her with one option: taking advantage of her personal network.

Through her social activism on body positivity, she had a fairly strong and engaged following. Sara wasn't shy about her desire to find her life partner and get married, and it was often a topic of conversation in her content and among her followers. Every few months or so, she would schedule a simple post with a reminder that she was looking to find her soulmate and calling on her network to help her out.

This is an example of one such post:

> Not going home for the holidays for the first time in a long time was actually a lot better than I anticipated, and I'm grateful for the circle of friends and my community that celebrated with me.
>
> During a conversation with the rabbi at one point over the holidays, he mentioned that he'd pray on my behalf, and I'm feeling pretty confident about my soulmate search...
> But, I do have to put in my effort and create that vessel into which G-d can easily drop Mr. Right.
>
> Many of you know me personally, many of you know me through my posts, but either way, I ask you to consider whether you might know of a single guy whom you think might potentially be a good match

for me. And once you're in that zone, think about any other single women or men you might consider setting up. And then do it! I challenge you to make one matchmaking related phone call or text today.

On that note, here's the scoop on me:

Sara used her social media network to her benefit—and to remind others that they can help their friends as well. And it worked. She did, in fact, get quite a few people reaching out to make suggestions and get more information from her. While none of those suggestions panned out, she claims it was still one of the best forms of networking she's done for her dating life.

You can do the same. Share as much or as little information as you feel is appropriate. (But don't forget that it's never a bad thing to push your comfort zone a bit.)

Online Dating Platforms

You're here reading all about virtual dating, so I'm going to make an assumption that you're probably already registered on at least one online dating site or app. Which is awesome! But do you know why you're on that particular platform?

I know I just spent a long time explaining why the bigger your network the better, but I'm going to contradict myself here and say more sites and apps isn't necessarily more helpful.

Here's why: You probably have a personal life. You probably have a work life. You probably have other things going on. And even if you're marriage-minded and focused on finding your soulmate, you shouldn't be spending all of your spare time on your soulmate search.

When you are signed up for many sites and apps, there's a good chance your phone will be pinging on a regular basis, which can easily distract you from everything else going on in your life. And that's not necessarily healthy.

Remember the fishing analogy? Having multiple fishing poles in the water is why I feel strongly that you should bring your in-person network to an online platform. I'm also okay with you being on two or three dating sites at a time. But here's where the other part of the analogy comes in. The quality of the water and what it holds is important too. In our case, this refers to the dating platform itself and the kind of people who are on it.

Of course, with every platform you're going to get a mix of people, and of course there will always be some bad apples...okay, a lot of bad apples. That happens. But beyond that, you want to make sure that the kind of platform you're spending most of your time on actually has the kind of people you're looking for.

For example, if you're marriage-minded and looking to find your life partner and start a family, Tinder is not where you should be hanging out. If you're Jewish and looking to find someone who shares your faith, you're going to have a better shot on Jdate.com than you would on atheistpersonals.net.

My point is, are you in the right place? Are you in the best place? Let's clarify why you are where you are. Use Part 2 of the exercise at the end of this chapter to figure out where you should be focusing your efforts.

By keeping things streamlined to the platforms with the best potential, you'll save yourself time, effort, energy, and possibly money.

Now that I've shared my advice and thoughts on navigating networking in virtual dating, I want to share something that's on my mind. At first glance, it may seem to negate everything I've shared in this chapter, but trust me, it doesn't.

I believe that there is a divinely determined right time when you will meet your right person. I believe it will happen whenever it's meant to happen and there is no way to know when that will be. That can be frustrating as it feels so out of your control. It can be comforting to know that your soulmate exists and is waiting for you just as you are waiting for them.

So why put in all this effort if it'll anyway happen whenever it's destined to happen?

I also believe that we have an obligation to put our best efforts into this process. We don't know which specific effort will yield the result that we're looking for, so we try our best by doing what we believe we should.

As my client Sara said in her Facebook post, by putting in this effort, you are essentially creating the vessel into which God can drop your soulmate.

Going back to the fishing analogy, God will or won't send fish to bite, but if there's no fishing rod in the water with bait on the hook, there's no way to catch a fish. And He designed the world in a way that seems to reward our efforts. So again, while He may or may not send a fish to bite on one hook, there's still a higher chance of catching something if there are more lines in the water.

I share all this because I want you to know that at the end of the day, it's helpful to remember that while your effort is important, I believe very strongly that you will find your soulmate (or your soulmate will find you) at the right time. So do make an effort, but try not to stress too much.

Takeaway: Your network can provide a wealth of opportunity. Connect to your offline people online, focus your energy on the sites and apps that give you the best shot, and don't lose faith.

Exercise: Build Your Network

Step 1: Expand your social media presence

Use the following memory jogger to help with making those online connections. List the person's name and the platform they're on. There's a decent likelihood that you won't have enough space here for your entire list. Don't worry about that. You can always continue writing on a separate piece of paper. This is intended to be a starting point.

Childhood Friends and Teachers

Name _____ Platform _____

Name _____ Platform _____

Name _____ Platform _____

Name _____ Platform _____

Name _____ Platform _____

College Friends and Professors

Name _____ Platform _____

Name _____ Platform _____

Name _____ Platform _____

Name _____ Platform _____

Name _____ Platform _____

Extended Family Members

Name _____ Platform _____

Name _____ Platform _____

Name _____ Platform _____

Name _____ Platform _____

Name _____ Platform _____

Former Work Colleagues

Name _____ Platform _____

Name _____ Platform _____

Name _____ Platform _____

Name _____ Plattform _____

Name _____ Platform _____

Personal Life (doctor, cashier, barista, manicurist, librarian, etc.)

Name _____ Platform _____

Name _____ Platform _____

Name _____ Platform _____

Name _____ Platform _____

Name _____ Platform _____

Step 2: Focus your sites/apps presence

In the following space, list the sites and applications you currently have a profile on, along with the reason why you chose to register there. If you don't have a good reason, or any reason at all, no worries. The objective of this exercise is both to encourage you to be intentional and to help you see where a change might be beneficial.

App/Website Name_____ Reason _____

App/Website Name_____ Reason _____

App/Website Name_____ Reason _____

App/Website Name_____ Reason _____

App/Website Name_____ Reason _____

Now, do some research on five to ten other dating sites and apps that could potentially be a good space for you to find what you're looking for. Write down whatever your research shows about the site, the kind of people that are on it, and who it's best suited for.

App/WebsiteName_____Reason_____

App/WebsiteName_____Reason_____

App/WebsiteName_____Reason_____

App/WebsiteName_____Reason_____

App/WebsiteName_____Reason_____

Of these sites you've researched, make note of the ones that will probably yield the best results for you. This is also a good time to decide whether any of the platforms you're currently on are really not serving you. Those sites are probably not worth your time and money.

List the top two or three sites that you want to focus on for the time being.

App/WebsiteName_____Reason_____

App/WebsiteName_____Reason_____

App/WebsiteName_____Reason_____

Of course, once you're registered with your top two or three sites/ apps, it's time to add your Hook and Soulmate Summary!

Chapter Six:
Mystery In Your History

"Somewhere between heartaches and waiting comes another chance to be found by someone that can show you that you are not just an option but the only choice."
–Unknown

Now that you've got a solid understanding of networking and how to use it to your dating advantage, it's time we talk about you accessing your own little black book of potential people to date. This chapter is where I teach you to be your own matchmaker and find a mystery in your history.

This Mystery in Your History exercise is one of my all-time favorites, and for good reason. Thirty-five percent of my clients who do it actually find their soulmate through this process!

In a nutshell, the way this works is that you list and explore all previous relationships to see if there could be someone there who is a potential date. And by all previous relationships, I'm talking about people you've dated in the past, but I'm also talking about elementary school and college friendships, neighbors and people you know from around town, travel buddies and work colleagues. And people you've thought about dating, but never did.

Some people really resist taking another look at relationships that didn't work out the first time. But the reality is that you are a different person now than you were then, and your dates probably are too. It could also have been that you dated the right person, but not at the right time.

It's worth taking a second look, even if you end up deciding to leave the past in the past.

The reason I encourage clients to go through this process is because a 35% chance of finding your soulmate is HUGE. That's better odds than any dating site, app, or matchmaker service you're going to find—by a wide margin. And why waste time looking into the future if your soulmate might already be in your past?

If you're rolling your eyes here, or don't believe that this is even worth trying, know this: every single one of my clients who did this exercise and actually ended up marrying someone from their past said to me, "Aleeza, there is nobody. I'm sure there's nobody." But I'm the coach, so they gave it a try just to humor me, and...voila! It works.

Actually, here's a fun story for you.

Rachel and I were on the phone, talking about the Mystery in Your History exercise. And she was not liking it. She actually fought me tooth and nail on making her list.

But she did eventually present me with a list that totaled 45 people. "Aleeza, I had to dig really deep for this," she said. I smiled and responded, "Perfect."

We went through the list together, nixing each prospective suitor one by one based on her research and explanations of why they weren't viable options.

"Okay, this one's married...this one disappeared off the face of earth—I Googled him and it's like he never existed...this one's married...this one lives overseas and I can't move because of my mom..."

We systematically worked through each name until I said, "What about this one?" and she responded, "Well, I mean, he's a good guy, I like him. I'm looking for somebody like him, but not him."

If you know me, you know I push back! So I challenged her. "Okay. Why? Convince me why it should be someone like him, but not him." She gave me a few flimsy justifications on why it wouldn't be a good idea, and I said, "Those reasons don't really invalidate him as an option. I actually think you should go out with him."

Of course she responded with the classic, "I was going to set him up with my friend." To which I said, "Don't. Instead say, 'I was thinking about setting you up with my friend, but actually, I'd rather ask if you'd like to grab a cup of coffee with me?'"

He said yes.

It's five years and two kids later and they're more in love than ever!

Obviously, completing this process isn't a guarantee that you'll find The One. But again, a 35% chance of finding your soulmate makes this a very promising and rewarding exercise.

It's funny, actually. People call me all the time to ask me if I have a Little Black Book of people I can set them up with. And I always tell them, "I don't. But you do!" This list is going to be your Little Black Book.

For the record, I don't need you to emotionally buy into this and be excited. I don't expect you to have butterflies in your stomach. I just expect that you're going to look at this list and really give it thought.

Alright, so what are you actually supposed to do?

It starts with a gigantic brain dump. Anybody that you ever dated (even if it didn't go particularly well), anybody that you ever thought about or wanted to date (even if they didn't want to date you), everybody that anybody ever told you to date, and all the other friends and acquaintances that you never even considered dating.

List them out, person by person, using the memory jogger at the end of this chapter for inspiration. Remember that there is no "correct" number of people to have on your list. It could easily be 50—or 350. It'll just depend on your personal network. Don't stress about not filling in all the blanks or needing more space.

Do not over-analyze whether or not to add a name to your list! There's absolutely no room for prejudgement on this list. Simply add anyone who comes to mind; you'll get to filtering through them later.

And know that you will likely not complete this list in one sitting. Start today, but give yourself at least a week to complete it.

Once you get all of those names down—awesome job, by the way!—it's time to sort through them all. And don't worry; just as in the first step, it's okay if this takes you more than one attempt.

Starting with the first line, review each name and put an "x" in the checkbox for anyone who is currently married. (Divorcees can stay on the list.)

Then put an "x" in the checkbox for anyone whom you once liked but now realize is not compatible with the current you (you have different values, they live overseas and you can't move, etc.). This will take some serious honesty. Look for an absolute reason to say no. If you're crystal clear it doesn't work for you, put an "x" in the box.

Once you've put an "x," make note of the reason in the space between the name and the checkbox. This will help you keep track of things as you move through this exercise.

Do not cross out any names because you think they do not like you. Time has passed and things may have changed. Maybe you went out a couple of years ago and it just wasn't the right time yet! Or maybe you thought they didn't like you but they actually did but just didn't know how to show it.

Do not cross out any names due to fear. Take a deep breath! We know how real the fears can be. No one wants to be rejected (especially a second time) or face an uncomfortable or awkward situation. But please leave that name on there!

Do not cross out anyone whom you simply don't feel like dealing with or looking into right now. You don't need to do anything you aren't ready for, but please leave those names there. Perhaps at a later time you may feel ready to pursue them if nothing else works out.

Once you've taken all the "x's" off the table, it's time to review the remaining names of available singles. Put a "✓" in the checkbox for anyone on this list whom you are definitely interested in.

If you don't know enough to decide that yet, you're not sure whether they're still married, or need to give it some more thought, put a "?" in the checkbox.

The question marks are for you to investigate and evaluate. You're going to ask yourself whether it's something to consider pursuing or not at all. Every question mark should, with serious thought and consideration, turn into an "x" or a "✓." If you come across a question mark that you don't really feel like looking into it, but you know you probably should, just do it. You want to be sure that this person isn't your 35%, that you're not passing up your soulmate prematurely.

Now, once you're done with the evaluation process, you may only have between one and five checks. Yup, from a list of 150 people, it's very possible that once all the filtering has been done, there are only four solid options. That's four more than you had before you began this exercise.

Which brings you to lights, camera, action time!

Leaving off any names that were nixed (all your "x's"), rewrite the list, organizing it in order of preference, priority and convenience. You can take into account their location, how easy it will be to contact them, and how you feel emotionally about doing so.

If getting in touch is difficult for you, that person should have a lower priority on your list. And somebody who is quick and easy to contact, right around the corner—they're going to rise to the top. If you're feeling nervous because you have a history, or you're not even sure whether they remember you, or you feel awkward, or you feel they're out of your league, remember that just as you've changed since you spent time with them, they have too. Maybe their life circumstances changed, or maybe their perspective changed, or maybe they never actually disliked you the way you thought they did. They might actually need your help in bringing the two of you together.

My point is you literally have nothing to lose!

So decide what action you will take this week to make contact with the first person on your list and reach out to them. Use the following space to record whom you reached out to, when, and what happened.

And if you are finding it hard to make contact with the person you have chosen, I recommend just moving on to the next person on your list. Don't get stuck!

Reminder, if they say, "No, for now," they don't get crossed off the list—it is not yet a hard no. Sometimes people are unavailable, busy with work, dating but in a bad relationship and maybe trying to get out. There might be a lot of reasons why somebody isn't available today, but it's not a no to you. It's just a no to the timing.

So if there's anything like that, leave them on the list and revisit it in one month. In the meantime, keep moving through your list until then, and hopefully, you will find a Mystery in Your History. If you do find one, email me. I want to know!

On a practical note, I know it can be a bit scary to just reach out and throw out the idea of dating, especially if you're currently friends and don't want to risk that friendship. To that, I suggest being straightforward. Let him or her know that you're interested in dating. If they are too, great. And if not, respond with a message saying that you still value their friendship and don't want to lose them over this. A true friendship will be able to endure a moment of discomfort.

If you're not comfortable with a head-on approach, it's also okay to send a more subtle message and gauge potential interest from their response. Saying something like, "I wonder what it would be like if we dated..." can either create an opening for them, or let them totally shut the idea down. The more you give them to work with, the more you can sense the situation. And it's okay if it takes a few conversations until you find the answer you need, be it a yes or a no.

Now once you've gone through this process of reaching out to the people on this list, one of three things will happen.

1. You'll date 'em and realize you've found your soulmate.
2. You'll date 'em, realize they're not for you, and move forward with other dating options.
3. You'll reach out to 'em all and none of them will be interested.

If the first option happens to you, woohoo! Mission accomplished.

If not, that's okay. At least you'll know that there isn't any mystery in your history. At that point, you really can say goodbye to the past and move forward with no looking back and no regrets. You won't be dealing with any of the "I wish I would have, I should have, why didn't I give it enough time," that so many others struggle with on a regular basis.

Takeaway: You are your own best matchmaker. Use the network you already have to connect with your soulmate.

Exercise: The Mystery in Your History

Step 1: Gather the Options

Note: For this step, just focus on putting the names down. Ignore the "reason" and box at the right side of the line. You'll come back to that in a little bit.

Using the memory jogger below, list anybody that you ever dated, anybody that you ever thought about or wanted to date, everybody that anybody ever told you to date, and all the other friends and acquaintances that you never even considered dating. Don't over-analyze! If a name comes to mind, write it down.

Childhood

Name_____ Reason _____ ☐

Name_____ Reason _____ ☐

Name_____ Reason _____ ☐

Name_____ Reason _____ ☐

Name_____ Reason _____ ☐

High School

Name_____ Reason _____ ☐

Name_____ Reason _____ ☐

Name_____ Reason _____ ☐

Name_____ Reason _____ ☐

Name_____ Reason _____ ☐

College/Grad School

Name_____ Reason _____ ☐

Name_____ Reason _____ ☐

Name_____ Reason _____ ☐

Name_____ Reason _____ ☐

Name_____ Reason _____ ☐

Vacation/Summer Camp

Name_____ Reason _____ ☐

Name_____ Reason _____ ☐

Name_____ Reason _____ ☐

Name_____ Reason _____ ☐

Name_____ Reason _____ ☐

Friends/Acquaintances You've Lost Touch With

Name_____ Reason _____ ☐

Name_____ Reason _____ ☐

Name_____ Reason _____ ☐

Name_____ Reason _____ ☐

Name_____ Reason _____ ☐

Family Friends

Name_____ Reason _____ ☐

Name_____ Reason _____ ☐

Name_____ Reason _____ ☐

Name_____ Reason _____ ☐

Name_____ Reason _____ ☐

Work Associates

Name_____ Reason _____ ☐

Name_____ Reason _____ ☐

Name_____ Reason _____ ☐

Name_____ Reason _____ ☐

Name_____ Reason _____ ☐

People You'd Like to Date

Name_____ Reason _____ ☐

Name_____ Reason _____ ☐

Name_____ Reason _____ ☐

Name_____ Reason _____ ☐

Name_____ Reason _____ ☐

Previous Dates

Name_____ Reason _____ ☐

Name_____ Reason _____ ☐

Name_____ Reason _____ ☐

Name_____ Reason _____ ☐

Name_____ Reason _____ ☐

Step 2: Eliminate the Nos

Review each name above, and put an "x" in the checkbox for anyone who is currently married. (Divorcees can stay on the list.) Then put an "x" in the checkbox for anyone who is not compatible with the current you. Once you've put an "x," make note of the reason in the space between the name and the checkbox.

Do not cross out any names because you think they do not like you. Do not cross out any names due to fear. Do not cross out anyone whom you simply don't feel like dealing with or looking into right now. If you have an absolute reason to say no, put an "x"—if not, leave that name for now.

Step 3: Check the Yeses

Review the remaining names, and put a "✓" in the box for anyone on this list whom you are definitely interested in. If you don't know enough to decide that yet, you're not sure whether they're still married, or you need to give it some more thought, put a "?" in the box. Every question mark should, with serious thought and consideration, turn into an "x" or a "✓."

Step 4: Make Your Shortlist and Take Action!

Name _____ Date _____ Notes _____

Name _____ Date _____ Notes _____

Name _____ Date _____ Notes _____

Name _____ Date _____ Notes _____

Name _____ Date _____ Notes _____

Decide what action you will take this week to make contact with the first person on your list and reach out to them. Use this space to record whom you reached out to, when, and what happened.

Chapter Seven:
Initial Interactions

*"Maybe it won't work out. But maybe seeing if it
does will be the best adventure ever."*
– Unknown

Do you ever feel like dating has a whole bunch of rules that you were never taught, and you're never really sure if you're getting it exactly right?

The truth is, it kind of does. But that doesn't mean you can't learn those rules and how to navigate them. That's exactly what we're going to go over in this chapter.

We're going to begin with the basics of starting a conversation online. But before we do, I want to talk about the goal of starting that conversation. We've already established that you're reading this book because you're marriage-minded, you want to attract quality dates, find your soulmate, walk down the aisle, and live happily ever. Right? To do all that, you need to start with a conversation.

Let's clarify, though, your ultimate goal here isn't simply to start a conversation. Your goal is to start a conversation that will lead to a date so that you can find out whether this person could potentially be The One.

And while messaging is a great start...it's just the start. So I want you to set a goal for yourself. From the time you start chatting with someone, aim to move the relationship to a phone or video date within 10 days. Yup, 10 days.

If you've got something going, this shouldn't be too challenging; and if what you've got going isn't going anywhere, then there's no reason to continue. This is the stage where potential dies easily. If neither of you makes a move within ten days to take this to a more personal level, that's pretty much a guarantee that it won't go anywhere.

Right about this point is when I usually get the question, "Who should do the reaching out?" Is it appropriate for women to reach out to men? Is it true that women want to be wooed and don't like it when men are straightforward?

The short answer is that these days everyone is reaching out to everyone, and if I were you, I wouldn't wait.

For those of you who want the longer answer, here it is.

Don't hang your hopes on the gender norms you're familiar with from the past. It's true that in real-life dating, women want to be asked out. But it's also true that nowadays women successfully ask men out all the time.

In fact, I like to reference Matthew Hussey's handkerchief theory when speaking about this. Matthew claims that women have been making the first move for centuries, all the while letting the men believe it was their own idea.

He explains that when a woman was out for a walk and a gentleman across the road caught her eye, she'd innocently drop her handkerchief. He'd notice, pick it up, rush to return it to her, and a conversation would be started. Hussey's modern example of this is when a woman and her friends are out, and she notices a guy at the bar. She goes up to the bar to order her drink, sets her jacket down on a chair, and when her drinks are served and her hands are full, she asks if he could help her out by watching her jacket for two seconds. He does, and when she returns to grab her jacket and thank him, she has an opportunity to unassumingly strike up a conversation.

Obviously, things are a little bit different online and being more straightforward is necessary. But, don't feel like this is "so modern" or "feminist" if you're more of an old school kind of gal. Women have been doing this for a long time!

Now guys, let's talk about whether women want to be chased. My take on it is that you have to find a balance.

Yes, women liked to be approached by a man who expresses interest. If he doesn't show any interest, there's no indication to her that he might want to get to know her, and so there's no chance of connection. If she doesn't think he's interested, she's going to feel less interested, and it's over before it begins.

However, when a man is overeager, she may find it unappealing or alarming. If the level of interest isn't mutual, it can be quite uncomfortable for her when he's significantly more expressive, and might have her backing away.

Finding that balance might be a bit challenging, but with practice, it's definitely doable.

For example, if you are interested in someone, send them a message. And then give them some time to respond. Don't send them a second text within minutes or even a few hours.

If they don't respond after 24 hours, you can text again, as they may have missed the text or just been caught up with work and forgotten to reply. If they don't respond after that second text, you shouldn't put in more effort at this time. If ever they should respond and you're still available, feel free to give them a shot.

So you have your 10-days-to-a-date goal in mind. The women are ready to start a conversation, and the men have practiced finding their balance. Now you open that app, find someone you're interested in, and send a message.

So what exactly should you say?

VIRTUAL DATING

Let me start by telling you what not to say. Do not ever start your message with "Hey, sweetie" or "cutie" or "doll" or "love" or "honey" or any other term of endearment that you have clearly not earned the right to use. He or she is not your anything yet.

While these expressions are often appropriate within the context of dating, they signify a certain level of intimacy. When you have not achieved that level of connection yet, they actually come across as rude, and to some people, offensive.

Honestly, it's like the online version of catcalling. Just don't do it.

Let's pause for a moment to acknowledge that it's possible you might have done this before. You might have thought it was cute, a good ice breaker, a sweet way of engaging with someone online. And if you have, that's okay. Now you know better. You don't have to give up on virtual dating forever; simply acknowledge your mistake and don't do it again.

Instead, I recommend that you start by actually using their first name, assuming it's listed in their profile. "Hey Michael," or "Hi Shaina." As simple as that. Then immediately add another personal comment based on their bio. By doing this you show them that this isn't some random message just because you're bored, but that you're actually interested in them specifically.

Obviously, you don't actually know anything about this person yet, so there's only so personal your comment can be. Do your best to personalize it using the information in their profile and your connection with it.

Sure, this will take more time than just churning out another "Hey, how was your weekend?" But it's a lot more likely to get a quality response in return. And from there you are much better positioned to get a real conversation going.

Once you have the conversation going, focus on asking open-ended questions. Open-ended questions are pretty much any questions that do not lead to a yes or no (or other one-word) answer.

This is so important because close-ended questions make it hard to keep the conversation moving. They are also what feed into that inter-view-like feeling, which is definitely something you want to avoid.

Open-ended questions leave a lot more space for other ideas to flow in, and for the conversation to move in different directions.

And when you're done answering a question that you were asked, don't forget to throw the ball back into the other person's court. You can simply ask, "What about you?" or you can put a twist on it so it doesn't become a stale back-and-forth of comparing notes.

Here are some examples of common first conversations—first with closed-ended questions that lead nowhere, and then an open-ended version.

Closed-ended (leads nowhere):

Hey Noa, how was your weekend?

> Good. Yours?

Pretty fun. Went to the beach with some friends.
Got some awesome photos.

> Cool.

Yeah.

Open-ended (leads to conversation):

Happy Monday, Noa! Can't believe the weekend is over!
I generally sit around and do a whole lot of nothing on Sundays, but this weekend I went to the beach with some friends. Had an awesome time and got some great photos. Want to see?

> Sure!

(Sends three photos: two of the ocean, one selfie.)

How did you enjoy your weekend?

65

> Mine was boring compared to yours, lol. Hung out with my cat and read - and finished - a novel I've been trying to find time to read for like two months now.

Haha, which one?

> Wuthering Heights by Emily Brontë

Never read it. You'll have to tell me more. What's your favorite part?

Closed-ended:

Good evening, Steve. I liked your profile and think we have a lot in common. Would you like to chat?

> Ok.

Nice. Where do you live?

> Toronto.

Cool, I'm Canadian too.

> Nice.

Yes, I live in Winnipeg. I see you like wine.

> I do. Do you?

Yes.

Open-ended:

Good evening, Steve. I just read through your profile and like you, I believe traveling is the best gift one can give and get. I kind of think of it as a wine tasting tour of the world. You get to explore places and try things you might not have done otherwise, in small amounts, without overwhelming yourself. Plus, you can literally try different wines. Which country that you've visited is your favorite and why?

Hi Elena, nice to meet you! I really like the wine tasting analogy. As a winemaker myself, I don't know how I didn't come up with that on my own. I've got to say that Italy is an all-time favorite. With the wine selection there, and the number of independently owned wineries, how could it not be? The truth is, though, it's not even the wine that draws me there. There's something about the culture that's so friendly and inviting, so family-oriented and traditional it really speaks to me. Have you been to Italy? Do you have a favorite memory from there? Yes, I hear the wine there is worth traveling for. No, I've never been to Italy, but I've been to France, and while the culture is so different...

Closed-ended:

Hi Naomi, this is Adam. I haven't dated online before, so I don't know how this works. But I like your profile and your picture is really pretty. I'm sure you get told that all the time.

Thanks.

You're welcome. So do you want to chat?

Open-ended:

Hi Naomi, this is Adam. I'm new to this online dating thing, so I hope you'll give me a chance to figure it out. I read through your profile and love that you're a mechanical engineer and work in HVAC. I actually studied engineering before becoming a firefighter. It wasn't for me, but I'd love to hear what you like about your job?

Hey Adam, no worries. There's a learning curve, but you'll get the hang of it soon enough :) I'm actually finishing out my last two weeks at my job before I leave overseas for a charity mission. Desk life isn't really for me. You can probably relate! I have something lined up for when I get back in three months with a different company with a more hands-on position. What drew you to firefighting?

That sounds awesome! I did a charity mission two years back when we went to California to help with the wildfires there. You know how every little kid wants to be a fireman when they grow up? Well, I was

67

no different. Except I was told that wasn't a real job. So I went to school, got my degree, and eventually realized I really wasn't cut out for that. My heart is in helping people on the front lines…so change happened :) What are you most looking forward to on your mission?

There's no better time to practice this than right now. So pull out your phone, sign into your account on any dating site and find a couple of people you would potentially be interested in messaging. You don't have to actually message them right now, but at least use the exercise at the end of this chapter to practice what you would say.

Start by putting down any of their bio information that really speaks to you, that you feel you can work with in crafting your message.

Next, write down what your go-to message would have been before you read this chapter. I want you to do this because it prevents you from accidentally writing that same message down this time around.

Lastly, come up with a personal greeting that invites them to engage back with you.

All that said, this is your reminder not to overthink any of this. If you're not familiar with this approach to messaging, it will take you some time to get the hang of it. And that's totally okay. But do not refrain from messaging people you are interested in because you're not sure if you'll get it right or not!

Please remember: not getting replies is not a fail. The only fail that could happen here is if you want to message someone but you don't.

I fully expect 90% of the people that you message not to respond to you. So let's say, for simplicity's sake, you message 100 people. I would guess about 10 of those will respond (but if it's closer to 7-8, that's still normal), and of those ten, you'll probably only be interested in 2 of them once you start to get to know them.

I share this with you because these are normal dating statistics, especially when you're dating online. So many people have accounts that they don't even remember exist. Others just ignore messages that don't appeal to them. Some intend to respond, get distracted by work or life or whatever else, and totally forget.

This is actually a good place to tell you my "99% Failure" rule, which is: you will fail 99% of the time in dating. By that, I mean that if your goal is to find and marry your one true soulmate, then every other person you match with, interact with or date until you meet your person will not work out. Things not working out with the person you're dating

Practice makes progress.

is not a bad thing! It just means you're now one step closer to The One.

My point here is, don't stress about the people who don't answer. Don't feel bad, don't take it personally. Focus your energy on the people who do respond.

Now, the only time where this does not apply is if you've sent about 25 messages and gotten zero responses. In that case, you should reevaluate the kind of messages you've been sending and/or the kind of profiles (i.e., people) you've been sending them to, and see if perhaps there's something you should change. If you're having a hard time objectively discerning what the issue could be, don't be shy about asking a friend for a second set of eyes. And then simply tweak things and try again.

Remember, the only possible fail here is doing nothing. So give yourself permission to fumble a couple times on your way to figuring it out. Know that you will likely send a few messages and then later, when you're doing something mundane like folding laundry or waiting for the coffee to brew, you'll suddenly come up with an incredible line that would have been so much better, and it'll feel like kind of a bummer that you didn't think of it earlier.

That happens to the best of us, and it's fine. Again, the more you implement this approach, the easier it'll be to come up with things to say and questions to ask, and the fewer mistakes you'll make. In the meantime, don't be afraid of *mistakes*. Practice makes progress.

And keep in mind that open-ended questions are not just for initial messages! You should be working on using this technique in all of your conversations moving forward, including any messaging that takes place via texting, and all phone or video dates as well. You and your date will enjoy the conversations more because of it!

Before we wrap up this topic, there is one more important point that I must mention. And I know this isn't particularly popular advice and you probably won't love it, but I promise it'll make your life easier and your dating experience more hassle-free.

So here it is: when it comes to online dating, more is not merrier.

In other words, you should ideally focus on dating one person at a time. I call this "monogamous messaging."

To be clear, it's realistic to assume that you will message multiple individuals until you start to develop a stronger connection with one.

How exactly do you decide who to continue dating and who to put on hold?

I advise focusing on the person who is most engaged with you and responds to your messages most consistently. There are a few simple reasons I recommend this.

First, with a responsive person, you'll be able to figure out more quickly whether they are right for you. And if it doesn't work out, you can go back to the people you were initially messaging and give it a go with the next one.

Second, speaking to multiple people at once can encourage unhealthy comparisons between the different people. I'd rather you compare the person you're dating to YOU and what you're looking for than to someone else you're dating.

Third, you start forgetting who you told what to you and when. Ever had a situation where you started off a story with, "I can't remember if I told you this, so if I did, just stop me..."? I certainly have. And while that's fine once in a while, it tends to happen a lot more often when you're in the initial stages of dating multiple people and you're just getting to know each other. That's not something we want. Plus, and potentially more awkward, you start to mix up THEIR stories! You reference a specific incident that you think Person A shared with you, when in reality, that was Person B's experience. Again, the more people you're dating, the more this happens. It's just not a very productive way of moving things forward.

And finally, discouragement and burnout happen at a much quicker rate when you're dating multiple people at once. This is because there's a strong likelihood that a few of them won't work out, and because you are grouping negative experiences, it can feel more demoralizing than the end of just one prospect would have felt. Remember, it's not a fail to try and not succeed. It's only a fail not to try at all. And I'd rather you avoid getting to a point where you're so frustrated that you don't want to keep trying.

If you're bored and use messaging many people to fill your time...find something else to do! Refer to your bucket list and see if there's anything you can cross off. Find a new hobby. Reach out to your friends and ask them if they want to hang out. But don't use dating as a time filler.

Okay, you're ready to focus on one person, and you know how to choose who to start with. But if you're starting out talking to several people, how do you know when to focus on only one? My suggestion is that the time to shine the spotlight on one individual alone is when you've successfully had a first virtual date and are planning a second. At that point, there's obviously some potential there.

When you do get to that point, it's important that you do not ghost the other people you've been talking to up till then. That's simply not cool.

Instead, be honest and upfront about the situation. Send them a message along the lines of:

"I'm on [insert dating site/app name] to find and develop a real relationship. I imagine that we're both speaking to multiple people through this process as we search for "the one." Right now, I've developed a closer connection with one person in particular and I'd like to focus on seeing whether that can go somewhere. To respect both you and me, I'd like to put this conversation on hold for the time being. If things change, I will definitely reach out and would like to continue this conversation if you're available at that time."

If you're really not an upfront kind of person, here's an alternative:

"It's been really nice chatting with you. Something came up in my personal life that I need to focus on at this time. I plan to reach out again once things settle down."

Again, this last one really isn't ideal, but it's still better than a full-on ghosting.

If you're reading this book, I think I can safely say that dating is a priority to you and you want to do it right. I'm sure that the people you're dating want the same. But they may not know what you know about best practices. So don't expect them to know all this intuitively, or to be following the steps above. If they mess up in the process, be forgiving.

However, you can share in a "this is what I'm doing" sort of way. Meaning, once you've hit that third date and haven't been chatting with any other singles for a week or so, and you feel it's important for you to share, you can say something like, "From now, I'd like to focus on seeing whether this can go somewhere." (Nothing more intense than that though—you don't want to scare them off! And don't let them know that you've already been doing this from after the first date. Don't share it retroactively. Just talk about the now.)

Lead by example. But don't expect or demand the same from them. Your job isn't to teach them how to—or how not to—date. Just focus on your choices.

Stephanie, a former client of mine who is currently planning her wedding, recently shared her story with me. And while it seems to contradict just about everything I've outlined in this chapter, I feel it's important to share anyway.

The reason I'm sharing it is because I believe that, as I mentioned earlier, God designates a soulmate for every individual and you will meet your soulmate at the designated time. Yes, you do have to put in your effort to create the space for God to send Mr. or Mrs. Right your way. And yes, you should learn and implement best practices for the different stages of virtual dating. But when all is said and done, you are human. You will likely make mistakes. Who am I kidding? You will definitely make mistakes. When that happens, don't stress yourself out about it. Acknowledge it, explore what you can do differently for next time, put it out of your mind, and move on.

Often we get so caught up in our mistakes that we wallow in them far longer than we should. Sometimes we even feel good about the fact that we're "punishing ourselves" for that mistake. But that gets you nowhere closer to finding your life partner—it doesn't serve you. So like I said, pick up, and move on.

Stephanie's story is pretty much a what-not-to-do checklist that worked out by fluke—or rather, by God's design—but I think you'll find it amusing and comforting in those oops-I-shouldn't-have-done-that moments. I want you to remember that mistakes happen and you can still meet your soulmate.

Last June I decided to take a dating break.

I was 27 years old and more than ready to find my Mr. Right, settle down, spend time together as a couple and then start a family. But I was also having an identity crisis of sorts. I woke up one morning with more questions than answers, and wondered where my values really lay. It had been so clear to me for so long that I knew exactly the kind of guy I was looking for…and suddenly I wasn't sure anymore.

And I didn't feel that it would be fair to subject some innocent young man to my intellectual shenanigans and lack of clarity about my life. So I decided to take a dating break.

I planned to take six months to soul search, seek answers—find myself, if you will—and then I'd pick up dating where I left off.

Except, there was one thing: I was lonely. I had recently moved across the country, had no social life and just wanted someone to hang out with. So I re-downloaded jSwipe.

jSwipe is not the kind of app I typically used for soulmate seeking. I mean, granted, a friend of mine did find her husband on jSwipe. And I definitely knew of several other couples who met via jSwipe too… but I was convinced they were flukes. jSwipe didn't work for regular people like me.

But it would be perfect for finding a friend to connect with, hang out with, pass time with. I swiped right on a bunch of guys. Most were duds. They either never reached out or didn't respond to my text. I wasn't super disappointed though. It wasn't like I had invested much hope in this.

Then, on July 22, 2019, I swiped right on a random guy. I don't know why I did it. His bio had nothing but a smiley face emoji, and I never swipe right if there isn't some intriguing, preferably intellectual comment. His picture showed that he was culturally different than I was, and I never swipe right if I know right off the bat that we're this culturally different. His picture was hot, but I never swipe right based on nothing but a picture alone.

But this time, I did.

Sooner than I expected, he messaged me: "Hey sweetie." I rolled my eyes. Really? I mean, I wasn't surprised, but really? Can guys not get any more creative than that?

I never respond to those kinds of messages, so I don't know why I did. I guess I was feeling a little feisty. No one calls me "sweetie" without knowing me personally and gets away with it. So I responded back: "Hey honey."

And then we started chatting. I don't really know how or why. But we did.

It was basic getting-to-know-you stuff and I quickly realized that this was not a guy I was interested in, even just for hanging out. He wasn't my type in so many ways. He was from a different country, with a different culture, and a different language. It was too much. Not for me.

So I ghosted him. I know, I know. Not cool.

But the next day, I found out that a good guy friend of mine, someone I had wanted to date, had just gotten engaged. I was excited and happy for him…but I wasn't sure how to feel for myself. It was like the door had firmly closed on that possibility forever and there was no going back. And I really wanted company and a little distraction.

So when he messaged me again, even though I hadn't responded to his last few texts, I decided to ask him if he wanted to see a movie with me. I made it clear that I was not dating at the time and not interested in a serious relationship. I made it clear that I just wanted someone to hang out with.

I thought we'd meet up at the theatre or something, but he insisted on picking me up. And five hours and one movie later, he dropped me off at home, both of us amazed by the fact that two traditional-leaning human beings met up on a non-traditional dating app.

So we "didn't date" for five weeks. Five weeks of chilling at the beach at night, drinking whisky and coke at a country bar, shopping for formal clothes for our night out at Atlantic City, and spending many late nights out just talking and being comfortable with one another.

Needless to say, we started officially dating at some point along the way, and seven months and seven days later, he proposed to me.

And for the record, it turns out that it was his first time using *jSwipe*, and he had no idea what he was doing! Translating a common opening line from his native language, "Hey, sweetie," was actually totally appropriate where he comes from, even though it looked awful in English.

Takeaway: You can't finish what you don't start. Focus on making that first introductory message engaging and inviting. And then streamline your attention and focus on one potential relationship.

Exercise 1: Build a Winning Message

First, put down any bio information that really speaks to you, that you feel you can work with in crafting your message. Next, write down what your go-to message would have been before you read this chapter (to avoid using it). Lastly, come up with a personal greeting that invites them to engage back with you.

Don't overthink it!

1. Potential date's bio content that speaks to me: _____

_____

_____

My previous message would have said: _____

_____

_____

My current personal, open-ended message:_____

_____

_____

2. Potential date's bio content that speaks to me: _____

_____

_____

My previous message would have said: _____

_____

_____

My current personal, open-ended message: _____

_____

_____

3. Potential date's bio content that speaks to me: _____

_____

_____

My previous message would have said: _____

_____

_____

My current personal, open-ended message: _____

_____

_____

Now it's time to practice...in real life! So use these messages and reach out to that person. Or, come up with alternative ones and send them.

Exercise 2: Spotlight on ONE

Once you've started implementing the approach of only dating one person at a time, I recommend that you use the space below to keep track of any individuals that you've connected with online. This way, you won't feel like you're back to square one every time something doesn't work out—you'll have all the info you need to reconnect right here.

Name _____Site/App_____

Notes _____

Name _____Site/App_____

Notes _____

Name _____Site/App_____

Notes _____

Name _____Site/App_____

Notes _____

Name _____Site/App_____

Notes _____

Chapter Eight:
Dating Dos and Don'ts

*"Want to learn how someone really handles frustration? Put them in a
long distance relationship and give them a slow internet connection."*
– Unknown

Josh couldn't understand why he wasn't progressing with the women
he dated. One after another they dumped him before he even got to a
third date.

When Josh reached out to me, he had recently matched online with a
woman named Kayla, who he assured me was "different from the others." She was sweet and passionate and ambitious and loved to road
trip just as he did. Josh was genuinely perplexed about why this pattern
was happening to him, and determined to prevent it from happening
again with his new virtual date.

He and I had a heart to heart about how he keeps in touch with his
dates between a first and second date. He shared how much he enjoys
texting as a way to build the connection and get things moving.

What he didn't mention is that he is an over-texter. He would text morning, noon and night, talking about anything and everything. What he

perceived as a legitimate way of cultivating a relationship, women felt was clingy and possessive. So they ran for the hills. They, understandably, weren't ready for so much chatting so early on in a virtual relationship.

So we reviewed the dos and don'ts of virtual dating. Though it wasn't intuitive to him, Josh is a quick learner and he began to recognize his over-communication and make changes.

I am pleased to share that he and Kayla are officially a couple.

Just as Josh did, many singles struggle to find an acceptable communication balance while virtual dating.

When you and your date are limited to virtual interactions, it's totally possible for things to start to feel stale—more so than with in-person dating. However, more communication doesn't necessarily mean you'll end up in a better relationship. It doesn't mean you'll like someone more. It may even mean you get bored of each other faster.

Therefore, I recommend that you set parameters for your communication. Intentional contact with proper boundaries will bond a couple and keep the momentum going.

Texting

Once you've established a connection with someone online and have texted your way to a first date, it's time to slow down with the texting. This will actually set you both up for the best possible outcome with virtual dating.

In the beginning, dates one through three, save the texts for quick messages here and there or for planning phone calls or video dates. No text schmoozing.

After the third date, it is appropriate to start texting more frequently to express interest and continue building a rapport in between your dates.

As a starting point, consider using your past texting habits to form your texting etiquette today.

If you were dating in person, would you normally text with your date during work hours? After work? In the middle of the night? Follow your usual texting habits, provided you're not a compulsive texter.

However, if you have been told in the past that you text too much, use this time as an opportunity to break old habits and work on texting half as much as you used to. Avoid over-texting just because you're bored. Just as I recommended for loneliness, I'd rather you bother a friend or relative than annoy your new date.

Over-texting is one of the biggest issues I come across in virtual dating. Just because you can text someone every night and all day long, that doesn't mean you should!

While texting can be a super helpful way to instantly communicate, texting too often can make a phone begin to feel like a leash. Texting can get overwhelming if there is constant contact. Many people also start to get bored or annoyed with someone when too many texts come too fast.

On the flip side, if you've been told in the past that you don't text enough, use this time as an opportunity to break old habits and work on texting more than you may be comfortable with.

Texting too infrequently can signify to the other person a lack of interest in them, a lack of interest in dating in general, or a lack of interest in a serious relationship. If you are really busy with work or struggle with making small talk via text, this is the time to work on that. Because if you don't, your date will likely make assumptions and move on.

Phone and Video

For in-depth conversations, video or phone calls are better options than texting.

As a dating coach, I've been working with my clients via phone for years. I have clients around the world, so I don't always get the privilege of meeting people in person. The phone is a great way to learn about someone without a visual distracting you. Getting to know someone through the sound of their voice definitely gives you a feel for who they are.

With that being said, the phone alone tells just one part of the story. It is important for you to interact on a visual level with your date. When dating virtually, video provides you with a way to do that.

For both of those reasons, I believe in a step-by-step approach to this process.

Ideally, start by phone. This allows you to get to know your date without focusing on their looks. Did you watch Love is Blind, the reality TV show where participants date one another through a wall over a period of ten days, never seeing each other until they decide whether or not to get engaged? It's a little like the real-life version of that. It gives you a chance to get to know them on the inside first, before you see the outside. Do you like this mystery person whom you can't see, but are beginning to understand and know?

Find commonalities on your first call. See where you have points of connection. Are you able to keep a conversation going without getting bored or tired of speaking to them? Yes? Great! Your next virtual date can move to video.

Video chatting allows you to see their smile, their expressions, and other forms of non-verbal communication. This adds another dimension to your connection with your date, and builds on whatever you developed by phone.

I do want to note here that sometimes a bad phone or video date doesn't necessarily indicate a bad match. It may simply be that the person you're dating isn't good with tech. It does not automatically mean that they don't like you.

I learned this from my own husband! We had a five-minute phone conversation between our first and second dates. Two of the five minutes were nothing but awkward silence. And that was with me, the girl who can make conversation with anyone!

To be honest, initially I thought he wasn't interested in me. Then I remembered that he was the one who reached out to me, so there must have been some interest on his end. Our second date proved two things: that we did have a connection, and that phone dates were just not his thing.

If you're interested in someone and they don't seem to be great by phone or video, then you may want to try to progress your virtual relationship to an in-person one more quickly. If that's not feasible, try to grin and bear the virtual dates until you can meet in real life. With time, as long as you're both making an effort, the two of you will learn how to navigate this process together in a way that works for both of you.

Timing

Be mindful of your timing when it comes to dates.

When finding a time for your virtual dates, schedule them for when you would go on a real date. Don't make it for 9:30 p.m. Some people like to go to bed, or at least start to unwind, by then.

Also, the time past 9:30 p.m. is what I call "the bewitching hour." That's the time when our tired brain and loosened guard allows us to get extra emotional, or maybe it's just harder for us to think straight and express ourselves clearly. I know my clients have certainly had moments late at night where they just can't find the words they're trying to say. Do you know what I mean? From what I've found in speaking with many clients, strange things happen at night when couples date.

If the time zones differ, do your best to keep the date early. However, I know that sometimes the reality is that it'll be late at night for one of you. In that case, make sure that you're properly set up for the date. In other words, don't just be chilling on your bed in pajamas. And if you've had a particularly long or challenging day and are feeling sleepier than usual, it's okay to reschedule your date for another time. I'd recommend you do that rather than speaking nonsense. Just make sure you give your date a heads up of at least a couple hours, and reschedule right away. You don't want them to think you're just playing games.

Additionally, with both phone and video calls, it might be a good idea to set a time limit, say around 45 minutes. This is not a set-in-stone rule, especially if you both are really connecting and want to continue talking.

In general, if talking for hours is your style and energy, I can't tell you that it's the wrong way to date; but for most people, it's not ideal. I'd much rather you break the first few calls down to shorter interactions. Afterward, if you still like each other, you can lengthen the calls.

By doing this, you are being sensitive to different personality types. People who are conflict avoidant won't tell you they want to get off the phone. Introverts often get fatigued after looking at a screen too long, even if it's your attractive, smiling face they're looking at.

You're also setting yourself up for success by ensuring that you prevent burnout both for you and your partner.

Once you've got something going, aim to go on three dates in ten days. This builds good momentum and helps couples to bond in the beginning of a relationship. Three dates in ten days will also help you to gain clarity in a short amount of time. (I have an entire chapter on this concept in my book Get Real, Get Married if you want to learn more.)

Communication

Regardless of what kind of date you set up (phone or video), when or how long it'll be, be sure to communicate this information to your date.

The last thing you want is for your date to be prepared for a phone call and then thrown totally off guard when you video call them and they're not ready to be seen on camera. Or for you to promptly hang up after 45 minutes without giving them a heads up, leaving them assuming that you were eager to get off the phone.

Always err on the side of over-communicating rather than under-communicating.

And if you find yourself in the situation where a go between is setting up the date, and you're not sure what to expect, don't be afraid to text your date and say, "Looking forward to speaking with you soon, ring me when you're ready," or, "Looking forward to our FaceTime call, see you at 7." Specify how you expect to connect.

In the event that you do get a surprise video call and you were only expecting a phone call, you don't have to answer the video call. Just call them back and let them know video doesn't work for you right now, but you'd love to chat by phone.

Privacy

As a general rule, you want to make sure that you're set up in a way that gives you total privacy for the duration of your phone or video date.

If you live alone, this shouldn't be an issue. If you live with a roommate or two, as long as you have your own bedroom, this typically won't be an issue either. If, however, you live with multiple roommates and actually share a room, or you live at home with other family members, or you are a single parent with kids in the house, finding adequate privacy can be challenging.

In these situations, I would say the easiest and simplest solution is to let those people know that you have a meeting and that you are unavailable during that time. Ask for quiet and give them a certain timeframe. This will hopefully keep them from interrupting your call because they know when to expect you back. You don't have to specify that it's a date if you don't want to. Then find an empty room, preferably away from any noisy areas, lock the door if possible, and focus on your call.

If you feel that you'll be disturbed if you stay at home, you can consider taking your call outside and going for a walk (more ideal for a phone than a video date) or sitting in your car.

Final Thoughts

Keep in mind that virtual dating is new for a lot of people. Most people are just finding their way. Assume that your dates aren't familiar with best practices, and make sure that you are prepared so you can best guide your relationship. Don't be afraid to take the lead in communicating and setting appropriate boundaries.

Takeaway: Take advantage of the best practices outlined here and implement personal boundaries in order to create space for a healthy relationship to develop.

Exercise: Identify Your Weak Spot

Of the different dating dos and don'ts listed in this chapter, which one do you struggle with most?

_____

_____

How can you implement the tips and strategies suggested here to work on that specific struggle?

_____

_____

_____

Chapter Nine:
Virtual Flirting

"Flirting is a woman's trade, one must keep in practice."
– Charlotte Brontë, Jane Eyre

It was 10:55 p.m. on a Wednesday night, and Jessica was on her way home from a girls night out. It was time to head home, walk the dog, shower and fall into bed. But first, she needed to stock up on some groceries, so she made a stop at Ralph's.

As she was picking out a semi-fresh bagel from the bakery section for tomorrow's lunch, a middle-aged man walked up to her and asked, "Do you know where the yogurts are?"

Jessica has a friendly face, so strangers coming up to her with questions was not an uncommon experience. She flashed him a big smile, dropped the bagel into her paper bag and replied, "Sure! I'll show you where they are." She proceeded to personally accompany him to the dairy fridge.

As they made their way over, Jessica kept up a stream of friendly chatter, her smile never wavering. When they reached the yogurt section, she pointed it out to him and they kept the conversation going for another few minutes after he asked her which flavor was her favorite and they compared notes.

But when this stranger asked Jessica for her number, she was genuinely surprised. She wondered what impression she gave him that she, a 23-year-old grad school student, would be interested in going out with this 50-year-old gentleman.

She politely turned him down, and that's when we spoke.

Jessica is a client of mine who, on a scale of 1 to 10, scores 11 in flirting ability. Because she's such a natural flirt and doesn't do it intentionally, she often doesn't realize how it comes across to other people. She fails to notice that her actions are sending the wrong messages to the people around her.

Through coaching, Jessica has learned that while being friendly is a beautiful trait, it often is expressed as flirtation (not a bad thing, by the way, which we'll discuss later), and knowing when to hold back is important.

So I'd like to ask you: how comfortable are you with flirting?

On a scale of 1 to 10 (where 1 is "I couldn't flirt to save my life," and 10 is super-flirtatious), where do you fall?

If you fall around 6 to 8, you're golden and you probably don't even need to read the rest of this chapter. (But obviously, I'd recommend that you do anyway because you never know what you might pick up.)

If you fall anywhere from 0 through 5 or 9 to 10 (or more), this chapter will offer you some guidance on how to flirt appropriately on your phone and video dates.

However, just to make sure where on the same page, let's first define "flirting," because it often has a negative connotation and I don't like that.

According to multiple dictionaries, "to flirt" is "to behave as though attracted to or trying to attract someone, but for amusement rather than with serious intentions."

The first part of this definition is great; the second part is not. In reality, flirting is actually a very healthy and necessary way to build a connection with another person. The implication that it is done without serious intention, when this is often not the case, is not one I appreciate.

I'd like you to reframe the idea of "flirting" by looking at it as a productive action rather than something purposeless that is done to, or at the expense of, others.

Flirting is a form of communication. Flirting tells someone that you have noticed them and that you want them to notice you too. Flirting communicates interest in the other person and invites them to engage with you on a more intimate level.

In general, flirting can take many forms (sincere, playful, physical, etc.) and how it's expressed will depend on the circumstances and the personalities of the individuals involved.

Flirting can be particularly helpful if you're one of those people for whom dating feels like an interview of sorts. By engaging your date in a more playful, fun way, you create the space for a more relaxed, less formal atmosphere.

When it comes to virtual dating, your flirting is limited to texting, phone conversations and what your date sees on screen. For this, your voice, physical movements and facial expressions are what you have to work with. Fear not, though—by implementing a few specific techniques you can go a long way with virtual flirting.

Texting

The most important thing to keep in mind when texting is that there is no tone or other non-verbal communication to pull from to provide context. As a result, there's a much higher chance of your text being misread and/or misunderstood.

This means that it's up to you to put extra thought into your texts and do your best to word them so that they won't mistakenly be read in a way that you didn't intend.

One way to do that is to stop and review your texts before you send them. Our brains work faster than our fingertips. So sometimes you tap out a message, hit send, and then realize that it didn't quite come out the way you meant to express it. Taking that extra two or three seconds before you hit send can go a long way.

Another way to help you balance tone and intention is through the use of emojis. Yes, believe it or not, emojis are a valuable tool in modern communication. Emojis can add emotion, dissipate tension, and give you space to share feedback or criticism without seeming harsh.

For example, adding a smiley face when confirming a date projects an image of you smiling in the mind of your date, putting a smile on their face and adding to the general mood. Adding a sleeping face and hug emoji at the end of a message saying that you'd been looking forward to chatting but it just got too late, and requesting that they reach out earlier next time, lets you set your standards and express disappointment while showing that you're not mad or upset.

The one caveat with emojis is that you must be aware of their most common uses. There are some emojis that are seemingly innocuous, but may have inappropriate implications. The last thing you want is to send the wrong sort of message unintentionally. Or, they may just not be what you think they are. Like the gesturing no emoji, where the woman is making an X with her arms in front of her body, that my friend has been sending to everyone thinking it's a hug. (For the record, it's not. There's an actual hug emoji.) If you're an emoji user, you're probably familiar with this. If you're not, a quick Google search can offer you a basic overview of emojis and their typical uses.

With that out of the way, just keep in mind that at the beginning you should avoid texting as a way of developing your connection until you've had three virtual dates. Once you're there and you know this is a relationship that has some potential, you can use texting to further develop what you already started via the dates. Just remember to find that balance of not too much and not too little, as we discussed in Chapter Eight.

Things to Text

The best approach to take when texting is to keep to one of the following three categories.

Playful and humorous
Personal and establishing connection
Referencing something they said

Playful and humorous

Keeping things fun and light is a great way to communicate, especially in the earlier stages of a relationship, without feeling the pressure to go too deep. It also lends itself to a flirtatious tone, which is a good thing. And, as with the emojis, it allows you to share something that you're not ready to express in a more straightforward way.

> It's a good thing you're not here or there's no way I'd get any sleep tonight. We'd just end up talking straight through till the morning.

Personal and establishing connection

Creating a link between you and your date adds an element of closeness which can help your relationship grow. Whether that's something simple, like realizing that you've lived in the same place, or more intimate, like connecting through challenges and life experience.

> I can totally relate! In my case, being a child of divorce meant I was being shipped back and forth between my parents every other week.

Referencing something they said

This shows your date that you were paying attention to him or her. It reinforces the notion that this person is meaningful to you. This category is equally applicable whether you're in the earlier stages of a relationship and are just getting to know them, or you're in the later stages of a relationship and are getting ready to take the next step.

> I saw this T-shirt and thought of you.

We don't know the backstory here, but they definitely had a conversation. Maybe about his love of donuts and dislike for the gym, or perhaps his ability to maintain a six pack while eating donuts. Whatever it was, this message is personal and clearly references something that he's told her about himself.

Non-Verbal Communication

Always be conscious of your non-verbal communication and body language.

How are you sitting right now? Are you looking and feeling at ease? Or are you uncomfortable and projecting body language that says back off?

First off, sit up nice and tall. Imagine you've got an invisible string secured from the top of your head to the ceiling. Pull your shoulder blades back and down. You should be able to do this without looking or feeling like you're stiff and immobile.

This position inspires confidence, and there's nothing we want you to express more on your date than confidence. (No, I did not say arrogance or aloofness. Just confidence.) It also creates space for you to project your voice well when you're talking.

Head movements can also communicate a lot to your date about your readiness to connect with them. If you are stiff and unfriendly, your date may not open up much. Keep your head and shoulders relaxed, and aim for flowing and comfortable body language. (Yes, you will have to find a balance between flowing and comfortable and shoulders back confident. You got this.)

Tilting your head to the side can indicate curiosity and further interest. Nodding your head up and down lets your date know that you get what they are saying and are an engaged listener. Even when you're super engrossed in what they're saying and totally focused on listening, make sure to let them know you're hearing them through your body language. There's nothing worse than thinking someone's frozen when in reality they were just focused.

While talking with or listening to your date, keep your body language and gestures warm and open. Crossing your arms sends a message of skepticism or disinterest, whether or not this is your intention. So even if you're cold or find that position particularly comfortable, for the sake of your date, don't do it. Show openness through your hand placement.

Try this. Next time you video chat with somebody you're interested in, sit with your arms by your sides and use open hand motions while you're talking. Or try resting your hand on your chin. Just be careful that this is not the "I'm bored" look where you're trying to hold your head up, but rather the "I like you and I want to know more about" you look.

If this is all too hard for you, or if you are just struggling to look comfortable and relaxed, think of someone you know who easily looks relaxed when you're speaking to them. Have them in mind as you try to position yourself. Use them as an internal guide to remind you of how to get comfortable on video. While you may not be comfortable at first, you will use the image of your friend and see if you can do what they do to look cool, calm and collected—and interested!

Facial Expressions

How your face responds to the things both you and your date share is an important part of keeping your conversation entertaining and engaging.

An expressive face utilizes multiple movements. Raised eyebrows, a dropped jaw, exaggerated blinks...these show you are an attentive listener. (Don't overdo it: don't move so much that you make them dizzy or make yourself feel like you're on stage. This isn't a performance, it's a means to connect.) More important, these reactions give your date tangible feedback that you are enjoying the conversation and them. Use these tools to help to build a bridge to a great connection.

They say that "the eyes are the window to the soul," and I'm inclined to agree. There is so much that is expressed and shared through simple eye contact. It can be incredibly intimate, or uncomfortable, or both at the same time. Eye contact inspires connection and vulnerability. I can't recommend it enough while on a video date.

Keep in mind that holding eye contact for too short a time (under 2 seconds) shows that you are uncomfortable. It leaves your date wondering if you're an anxious dater or simply don't like them. On the other hand, holding eye contact for too long (over 10 seconds) can be intense and scare away a date. We're looking for balance.

Healthy eye contact varies between looking at someone (for 3 to 5 seconds) and then looking away. As your relationship grows you can increase that time and then even practice looking longingly into their eyes without speaking.

Use your smile to your advantage. When you smile, it lets your date know that you're enjoying their presence. (Well, virtual presence.) A smile signifies that you feel good in this moment, which implies that you feel good connecting with them.

Don't be shy about practicing with yourself before your date! Stand in front of the mirror for a moment and tell yourself a story about something that happened to you today. Watch your face as you talk. Do you find yourself expressionless or expressive? Did your eyes get bigger as you mentioned something unexpected, or did you raise one or both of your eyebrows when you got to that moment of skepticism?

Do a self-evaluation on how engaging your face is. Get to know the expressions that will catch someone's eye. And then practice. Talk to yourself in the mirror for five minutes a day, or record a video of yourself reciting a speech or acting out your favorite movie scene.

Master Your Voice

The biggest vocal mistake you can make is falling into a flat, monotonous voice while talking to your date. Booor-ing.

Make sure to vary your pitch, tone and volume, as these tools help you communicate in a more interesting and engaging way.

Look to create a moment with your vocal expression. Pause to create suspense. Take a deep breath for effect. Whisper a word for emphasis. You might even consider changing voices when relating a story involving other people.

And don't forget about laughter! I'm talking about a good giggle, not a nervous laugh. Laughing at the right moment can really put you and your date at ease.

Conversation

The very first moments of your conversation should be open, friendly and engaging. Don't wait for the conversation to progress to an arbitrary point before you turn on the charm.

Start lightly and increase your connection as you get to know one another. Pace yourself and don't come on too strong. Remember, it takes time to build a good connection, but you'll never get that chance if you don't catch their attention on the first date.

As with texting, keep in mind that you're aiming to include one (or more) of the following in your early conversations: humor and playfulness, personal connection, referencing something they said.

With that said, too much energy or using all of these flirting tools at once may be too much. You can come across as overeager, aggressive or obnoxious. If you are at a flirting comfort level of 10, turn down your energy to bring out the energy in your date. You don't want to overwhelm or overshadow them!

Cutting back a little will give them space to bring themselves out of their shell, and if you're flirting right, they will take advantage of this time to be open and excited with you in return.

Similarly, if your nature is to be open and friendly all the time, your personality can be misunderstood at times. Like Jessica, I've had clients tell me, "But Aleeza, I wasn't flirting, I was just being my friendly self." If you're on a date with someone and are not interested, your flirtatiousness might send the wrong message. So if you are naturally flirty and not sure if you're interested yet, you may need to dial back to a level 4 or 5.

If you understand these ideas in theory but in reality you can't yet make a shift, consider finding a coach or therapist to help draw out your best self and empower you to become more alive on your virtual dates. Research who is good in your area, or search for someone online. Three to four virtual sessions should be enough to help you implement change.

If you connected online with someone who appears to be a natural flirt and you're not sure whether they're genuinely interested or this is just their natural state, the truth is that you probably won't have clarity at first. To get a sense of where you stand, you could playfully say something along the lines of "Oh, you say that to everyone," and gauge their response. The people who are flirty with everyone will probably just laugh it off, whereas the people who aren't will usually deny the charge and then follow up that they really mean it.

On the flip side, if you're dating someone who is not a natural flirt, and you're not sure whether they're into you or not, the basic rule is that if they talk to you and keep talking to you, they're interested. If they become unavailable, they're not open to connecting with you. This will usually make things clear even with people who are not expressive about their feelings.

One final thought. The best atmosphere comes from you being you! You definitely don't want to show up online as a muted version of yourself. Whether you're the kind of person who's typically a bit shy and nervous at the start, or you just want to prep yourself so you can give your date your best shot, I suggest getting physically energized.

A great way to do this is by taking a quick jog around the block (nothing too intense, you don't want to show up sweaty and out of breath) or grab a cup of coffee about thirty minutes before your date begins. The movement can get endorphins flowing and the caffeine can really kick your energy levels up. Either method (or both!) puts you in a positive and attentive state for your date.

Takeaway: Flirting is an invaluable tool that can positively impact the development of a relationship. Know your flirtation level and whether you need to tone it down or kick it up a notch.

Exercise: Flirt Awareness

Take this moment to score yourself on a scale of 1 to 10 on the flirtatious scale. If you did this at the beginning of the chapter, just make note of your score here. If you didn't, do it now.

—— —— 2 —— 3 —— 4 —— 5 —— 6 —— 7 —— 8 —— 9 —— **10** ——

Remember that the goal is the zone of 6 to 8 for dating. If you're a 9 or 10 (or, like Jessica, off the chart), think about how you can lower that energy. If you're a 1 through 5, think about how you can raise it.

Use the space below to record your thoughts about your current state of flirtatiousness, and make any notes on what practical steps you can implement to bring you back into that sweet spot of 6 to 8.

_____

_____

_____

_____

_____

_____

_____

_____

Chapter Ten:
Meaningful Moments

"I define connection as the energy that exists between people when they feel seen, heard, and valued; when they can give and receive without judgment; and when they derive sustenance and strength from the relationship."
– Brene Brown

Do you ever have those moments where you like the person you're dating, but you just don't feel connected? Like there's so much potential, but just no spark of connection?

Mike did. He shares, "While on a date, I used to think about whether or not I was feeling connected. If I was feeling connected, great. If I wasn't feeling connected, I kinda gave up and watched the date go south."

Mike's experience is not uncommon. In today's day and age, many of us have the bad habit of experiencing events externally. We often view the moment through the lens of a discerning eye—judging the moment instead of remaining present through it.

Mike didn't accept this status quo. "However, I learned through coaching (and many bad dates) that my time was better spent when I was focused on helping my date feel comfortable and connected to me. Checking in with my thinking and feelings was best left for the post-date evaluation."

I couldn't have said this better myself! I often remind clients that you just can't rush the process. The way to build a meaningful connection is one moment at a time.

The goal of a first date is to get to the second date. The goal of the second date is to get to the third date. And so on. Staying present in the moment gives your budding relationship the time it needs to grow roots. And strong roots are the foundation to any meaningful connection.

As a dating coach who works with singles from across the globe, I have not had the privilege of meeting most of my clients face-to-face. Yet, we have a solid bond built on trust, a meaningful connection, and an understanding of one another. We've developed solid relationships virtually. I know it's not the same as building a virtual romantic relationship, but this advice is good for dating, business and life.

Coming into a relationship with the right attitude and expectations (and a solid internet connection!) is key to your success. It begins with you believing that virtual dating can work for you and that you have the tools and skills you need to be successful via this dating approach.

The good news is that when you believe that this can work for you, you can learn how to create a meaningful connection. Let's break things down to three basic principles.

1. Connect With Curiosity

Betsy was talking to Sam. Actually, Betsy wasn't saying much. She was asking the questions and Sam was doing all the talking. After the conversation though, Sam felt closer to Betsy and even thought she was an interesting person. He felt like they had a connection and wanted to get to know her more.

How did this happen? Betsy asked Sam lots of questions about good times in his family life, about his career choices, about his favorite memories...and then listened as Sam shared.

Sharing personal experiences, thoughts and feelings fosters connection. As a result, Sam was feeling closer to Betsy. And as long as Sam reciprocates with questions of his own and creates space for Betsy to share too, their relationship has potential.

When you're talking with someone, your questions should come from a place of authentic curiosity. Don't ask surface-level questions just to keep a conversation going. This isn't an interview.

The questions you ask should serve a purpose: getting to know and understand the person that you are dating. Ask questions that genuinely interest you and that you believe will offer you insight about your date. To be clear, these do not have to be existential questions about the meaning of life, and you don't have to delve into their childhood experiences right off the bat. You can still get to know a person through light conversation topics.

Think about the examples I shared in Chapter Seven. Through a few initial interactions, we learned that Noa likes to read classic novels, Steve is a winemaker who appreciates culture and is drawn to the traditional, family-oriented lifestyle he views in Italians, and that Naomi is taking three months off for an overseas charity mission. We discovered all these through a few open-ended questions. With each passing date, you can dig a little deeper. Don't jump all in right away.

When you're the one responding to questions, don't share facts, share stories!

For example, telling someone what you do is simply a piece of data. Even if they only asked what you do, don't give a simple answer. Remember, the way to a meaningful conversation is to share meaningful things. Not everyone is an excellent conversationalist. If you wait for the right question to be asked you may be waiting a long time! The person across from you might not have read this book, so they might not know to ask open-ended questions—but they want to get to know you even if they don't know how to ask in the best way possible.

So pretend they asked an open-ended question when you're answering. Sharing why you enjoy your work, or how you got into this field, is a lot more meaningful than simply saying you're an accountant. Knowing that Adam from Chapter Seven studied engineering, but gave it up to pursue his childhood dream of becoming a firefighter, is so much more meaningful than just knowing that he's a firefighter.

Here are some open-ended replacements to a few common first-date questions.

Instead of "Where did you grow up?"
ask "What did you like most (or least) about your hometown?"

Instead of "Have you experienced challenges that have shaped who you are?"
ask "What is the greatest challenge that you've had to overcome and how has that shaped who you are today?"

Instead of "How many siblings do you have?"
ask "Where do you fall in your family and how did that influence your relationship with your siblings?"

Help your date open up by asking intriguing questions like, "What was the best conversation you've had this year?" Or "If you could repeat any single day in your life, which day would you most love to repeat?"

The goal of any great question is to help someone open up and share a story. Stories are the glue that binds couples together.

Remember how Mike was so busy focusing on whether or not he was feeling connected that he was actually taking himself out of the moment? Using questions that put the attention on your date actually helps keep you present. Instead of thinking about your mental checklist and comparing whether they match up to it, focus on asking questions that help you get to know them better.

Leave all the other thinking for after the date.

Want more fresh, open-ended and engaging questions to ask on your date? Head to the Resources page of www.marriagemindedmentor.com for more.

2. Make Them Glow

Bring out the best in your date.

You can do this by asking questions that highlight their strengths and give them space to share information that puts them in a positive light.

You can also do this by genuinely complimenting them. I strongly recommend choosing compliments that focus on their inner value, on the things they embody and represent by choice. Meaning, rather than complimenting someone's eye color, compliment their response to a challenge they shared, or the compassion they expressed in a specific story they told you.

I'm not saying there's never a place to tell a woman she's beautiful or a man that he's handsome, but I'd prefer you offer a physical compliment such as "I love that new hairstyle" or "Your tie really brings out the blue in your eyes." In both of these, even though the compliment is physically oriented, it still addresses their input rather than just a gift that was given to them.

In dating coaching, I help my clients focus on bringing out the best—not only in themselves, but also in their date. When you emphasize the best in your date, they will respond and want to bring out your best as well. So instead of worrying how you're coming off to the other person, just focus on how you are making them feel throughout this date.

3. Understand and Accept

The third and most important way to make a meaningful connection, on-line or off, is to understand and accept everything about the other person.

You don't have to like them, but you can fully accept and understand them.

The bottom line is that you can't connect with your date if you're not taking the time to understand and accept who they are. If you just connect with your vision of who you want them to be, or who you think they are, you're not actually connecting with them.

By taking the time to get to know them—to learn what makes them them, to accept that they have strengths and weaknesses, gifts and flaws—you can then decide whether they actually might be a potential partner for you. Without doing that, though, you're connecting with a version of them that's been adapted by your brain to suit your interests, which leaves you with no insight into how suitable they are for you.

And even if this person is not your person, having the clarity to look at them and totally accept them as they are will allow you to make a meaningful connection which will help you determine what the next step is (say goodbye and move on, set them up with a friend, etc.).

Even with all the meaningful moments you'll experience with your date(s), and with all the intention you put into successfully dating, you will still have awkward moments. And that does not mean you're doing anything wrong!

Awkwardness in dating is normal. In fact, for the record, married people still have awkward moments too. You have them in regular day-to-day life...and relationships are a part of day-to-day life. I would say while dating, the 80/20 rule applies, where it's not unusual to feel that awkwardness about 20% of the time. Once you move toward marriage and your relationship grows deeper and solidifies, that 20% should drop down to near 5%.

Remember this: connecting virtually in a meaningful way is totally possible. My coaching happens mostly over the phone and has been pretty successful. You can be successful too, when you are looking to make the most of your virtual dating life.

Takeaway: You can absolutely develop a meaningful relationship online when you set out to do so intentionally and purposefully.

Exercise: Praise Practice

Think of a few non-physical compliments that you can offer a date. I suggest you think of a current or former date just to have someone in mind. We're conditioned to revert to the easy, "You look great," so this is a good opportunity to flex those complimentary muscles and get some practice. Think of a scenario where you could have complimented someone. Jot down the context and then the compliment that would have been perfect for that situation.

Context _____

Compliment_____

Context _____

Compliment_____

Context _____

Compliment_____

Chapter Eleven:
Distanced Date Ideas

"I exist in two places, here and where you are."
– Margaret Atwood

Virtual dating can get stale fairly quickly...if you're doing it wrong.

Nowadays, there are so many great ways to engage with your date online that even if you want to spice things up and do something more exciting than talk on half of your dates...you can!

Some of these activities are better for the earlier stages in the relationship and others are better for once you've developed a more intimate relationship. While I didn't specify which is for which because that is somewhat unique to each person, I trust that you'll make a good judgment call on what to do when. And, as always, if you're not sure, ask a friend or a dating coach.

Here are some of my favorite distance dating ideas.

Dinner Date

The variations on the kinds of dinner dates you can set up and have are endless...but here are my two favorite ideas.

1. Get your chef's hat on and cook it together. Decide in advance what your menu will be so that you both have time to pick up all the ingredients you need. At the scheduled time, hop onto

a video call and walk through the cooking process together. This is a fun way to make eating dinner alone a lot more exciting and entertaining.

2. You might not be able to take your date out to dinner, but that doesn't mean you can't take dinner to her. This is obviously more for special occasions, but it is definitely memorable! Mail out (or email) an invitation in advance, inviting her to an upscale virtual dinner date on a specific date at a specific time with a specific dress code.

Have dinner delivered from her restaurant of choice. In addition to that, send her a personalized packaged "dinner in a box" kit. You can really get creative here and go as personal as you want, but start with the basics—a couple of romantic candles, a wine glass and bottle of wine, a personal card—and go from there. Personally, I'd put in a little tablecloth with matching napkins, and some knickknacks that represent different aspects of your relationship.

Virtual Gaming

As with dinner, there are so many ways to approach virtual gaming. Here are two of my favorites.

1. HedBanz, Scrabble or any other interactive games that can be played via an app. I love a good ol' board game, and the fact that most of them are now available online opens up opportunities for social interaction and dating. There's something fun about getting to see the competitive side of your date and how seriously they take their gaming skills.

2. Whether you're an escape room junkie or have never even stepped foot in one, an online escape room is an awesome option for escape

roomers (did I just make up a term?) all across the board.

Similar to playing a board game together, this will bring out a playful, competitive side to your date (or you'll learn if they're just not like that), but instead of playing against them, you'll actually get to work together to come up with a solution and escape the room.

Explore the World

Although there might be hundreds, if not thousands, of miles between you and your date, you can still travel together. Virtually. There are many museums, monuments, and other incredible spaces that are now available to tour online.

From the San Diego Zoo to the Great Wall of China, from the Louvre Museum to Buckingham Palace, your options are many. Google has got a whole database of arts and culture related learning you can do together. Even cooler than both of you exploring separately from your phones or computers, Zoom screen share offers you the possibility of literally exploring together while chatting through the process.

Study Buddies

Okay, I don't literally mean study buddies in the context of school (although, I won't stop you if you like that idea), but if you've ever thought about learning a new language, or signing up for a course just because you thought it would be cool, now you can do that with someone else. Coursera, Kahn Academy and Duo Lingo are a few great places to start, but there are so many online universities that offer free classes.

Along these lines, you could also watch a TED Talk together on a topic that interests you and then discuss it. I find that a lot of my clients genuinely enjoy the kinds of conversations where they get to explore a topic that may not necessarily have come up on a typical date, but through the use of a TED Talk, they actually learn so much about the other, the way they think, and their perspectives on the world and life!

Love Language Quiz + Share

The Five Love Languages by Gary Chapman is a must read. Human nature is to give love just as we like to receive it. The problem with that is that your partner may not like to receive the way you want to give. In his book, Chapman outlines the five ways to express and experience love between romantic partners. They are (1) words of affirmation, (2) acts of service, (3) receiving gifts, (4) quality time and (5) physical touch.

I highly recommend reading this book (you and your date can even make your own mini book club!), but for your actual date, take the "learn your love language" quiz for couples. Complete the quiz separately and share your notes. Talk about what you've learned about each other and how you can implement this newfound knowledge into your future dates.

If you want to take it one step further, spend the rest of the date (or your next date) preparing something that your date would appreciate based on his or her love language. For example, a personal poem for someone whose love language is words of affirmation or a handmade coupon booklet with coupons they can cash in for someone whose love language is acts of service. There are lots of awesome ideas floating around the internet.

Paint Night

You don't have to go to a studio to paint, you can do it from home! Paint nights are a great outlet for creative expression and the best part is that you don't actually have to be an artist, or even know what you're doing. YouTube has a whole collection of step-by-step painting videos, including everything from picture painting to fluid art to dot painting.

You can either both pick up all the supplies you need, or you can send your date a personalized paint night kit, just as you would the romantic dinner date listed above. And at the scheduled time, you'd video your way through your shared painting experience.

Camp In

What sounds better than a fire pit, hot cocoa, and marshmallows? All that and no mosquitoes!

Create a mock campfire and share your experience virtually. If you've got a fireplace, get it lit; if you don't, you can put a YouTube video of a cozy fire on your laptop...or just pretend that it's there. Turn out the lights and snuggle under a cozy blanket with that cup of hot cocoa and marshmallows.

Have a ghost stories contest and if you're feeling techie, try adding sound effects to upgrade your storytelling skills!

Apartment Show and Tell

This is the one that I love most! Invite your date to virtually visit your home and show them around in a more intimate way than you would your average guest.

As you walk through the rooms, share with them your most sentimental item, your most expensive knickknack, and the most visibly worn piece of clothing you're still comfortable wearing outside. Have your date do the same. Choose different objects you see and ask them about the story the object would tell if it could speak. Talk about what memories the walls hold. There are so many great ways to get creative and personal with this one.

Along similar lines, you can photo share folders with pictures of different trips and experiences you've had over the years, and then look through the photos together as you tell the stories.

Takeaway: Being stuck at home is not reason to be confined to boring dates! With a little creativity, the world is still at your fingertips.

Exercise: Build Your Next Virtual Date

Alrighty, now it's time to make it happen! If you already have a date scheduled, start brainstorming for that date. If you don't, do this exercise anyway and you'll have something ready for when you do get a date on the calendar.

Using the list above, pick your top 2 or 3 date ideas, mark them down and then make note of any supplies you need to purchase or things you need to set up in order to make them happen. This way, when the time comes, you won't be scrambling to put it all together, you'll just flip to this page and have an exact plan of what needs to get done.

1. Date idea: _____ Supplies to purchase/Things to prep: _____

_____

_____

_____

2. Date idea: _____ Supplies to purchase/Things to prep: _____

_____

_____

_____

3. Date idea: _____ Supplies to purchase/Things to prep: _____

_____

_____

_____

Do you have a favorite virtual date that I didn't include in this list? We'd love to hear from you and share it with our readers! Email us at *coach@marriagemindedmentor.com* to submit your idea.

Chapter Twelve:
From Virtual to IRL

"Long distance relationships are hard, but they're also incredible.
If you can love, trust, respect, and support each other from a distance then
you'll be unstoppable once you're physically together."
– Unknown

If you're a Type A personality, you may be bothered by the fact that you don't know when you two will be able to meet "in real life" (IRL). There are so many possible factors at play here, including work, family obligations, distance, and finances, among others (including, you know, pandemic status!). But the truth is, you don't need to know exactly when or how an in-person meeting will happen.

Focus on building a rapport virtually. If that goes well enough and you both buy in, then you'll both be motivated to meet. The logistics and details will work themselves out. Trying to meet up might be a little complicated, but try to embrace the challenge that love brings. What a great problem to have!

Here are my thoughts on the who, what, when, and where of meeting up in person.

It's always ideal to meet in person as soon as possible. Obviously, that's not always an option, but I want you to keep this in the back of your mind. Sooner rather than later is better.

When I coach clients dating locally, I recommend that they meet within three weeks. Under extenuating circumstances, that timeline jumps to six weeks. With virtual dating, I would put that max at three months.

If you can't meet within three months, you won't be able to effectively progress your relationship. It's simply not worth the emotional investment and time commitment required to keep dating with no plan to meet in person. Additionally, if you do choose to continue dating virtually, there's a much higher chance of things actually being called off—not because this is a relationship that couldn't work for you, but because it lacks that necessary in-person connection.

Keep this in mind when you match with someone and begin connecting. Plan to meet within a three-month timeframe. And if it comes down to it, and you realize that it's just not going to happen, I advise you to put things on hold until you know you'll be able to meet. This way, you won't unintentionally sabotage the relationship. Plus, there's the added benefit that the distance may actually be a strong motivator for helping you figure things out and make an in-person date possible.

In the case of virtual dating, if you've had three successful virtual dates (ideally within that ten-day timeframe), you're ready to bring up the idea of meeting in person. That might be an immediate option, or something to talk about for a future date.

As a general rule, I believe that the man should offer to travel to the woman's location. If both parties decide it's more practical and convenient for the woman to travel, I suggest that the man offer to pay for at least part, and ideally all, of the cost of transportation.

Now, before you slam this book shut and accuse me of being old fashioned, I want to explain something. Men are protectors by nature and providing is a big part of the protecting game. No, this does not mean that women are lacking the giving gene or can't also contribute. But I do feel strongly, especially at the beginning of a relationship, that the man should offer to pay for dates (and, in this case, transportation), and that the woman should create space for him to do so.

What I've noticed after working with hundreds of dating singles is that when women don't allow men to give...the men find someone else to give to. Take some time to let this percolate if you need to, but keep in the back of your mind.

Now, let's assume that all is going well, you planned an in-person date, and you're getting ready to meet your date in real life for the first time. What should you be thinking about? Here are my top six things to focus on as you prep for a successful transition from virtual dating to in-person dating.

1. Be yourself!

No, seriously, be yourself. It can definitely be a little disconcerting to know that you're meeting someone who, on the one hand, knows you really well—and on the other hand, has never met the "real life" version of you. You might feel like your date knows so much and at the same time knows so little. You might be tempted to dull aspects of yourself that don't necessarily come through on video and highlight the aspects of yourself that do.

But I'm telling you: don't do that. Don't overthink it. You want this person to see all aspects of you—the ones they're familiar with and the ones that they're not. This might feel a little weird, but in a way, you're each getting to re-know each other with the goal of seeing if this can become a long-term relationship that turns into a marriage. The only way that can happen is if you present all of yourself fully.

So be authentically you. If you're not, your date will notice, you will notice, and it will be unnecessarily awkward. Also, authentic you is great—share it!

2. Don't worry too much about your perceived physical flaws or imperfections.

When it comes to physicality, although video provides a 2D experience, there's obviously a lot that can be easily hidden. This can include anything from your weight to your freckles, and it's completely normal to be nervous about how your date will react to seeing you in real life.

Obviously, as human beings we care what other human beings think of us. Especially when said human beings are people we care about. At this point in your relationship, your date means something to you, and it's important to you that they like you and are attracted to you. So it's normal that you care.

But don't get caught up in those insecurities. The reality is that they likely won't even notice whatever it is that bothers you so much and/or they don't care nearly as much as you do.

In fact, there's a high probability that they're feeling the same way! They probably don't even have the headspace to notice what's bothering you because they're worried about what you're noticing about them.

Does anyone else sometimes wonder why this has to be so intense?! Seriously though, feel however you're feeling, acknowledge your emotions, and then move past them. Don't get stuck in your insecurity.

If you have a history of doing just that and are afraid that you might be so worried about it that you'll be too distracted to be fully present, prepare a couple of tools in advance to help you stay in the moment. It can be anything from a piece of thread tied to your wrist that reminds you of your goal (to connect with this person you've developed a connection with) to reminding yourself, whenever you start worrying about what they're thinking, that they're doing the same.

3. Manage your own expectations.

Your expectation should be this: "I met someone virtually and this has potential, nothing more and nothing less." You'll also need to balance how you imagined this person would be with the reality, and there will almost always be some differences there, as we discussed in #2.

Focus on making one another comfortable, recreating the positive energy that existed online, and having a solid give-and-take in your conversation.

Now that you can see one another, you need to build on this momentum instead of letting it drag on. Make it a priority to see each other three times in ten days, and really get to know them. Because you have already established the relationship's foundation online, there's a good chance you'll have clarity about whether this is a potential match or not within those three dates. That's not to say you must make some huge decision, but if it's a definite no, you'll probably realize sooner rather than later.

4. Remember that your brain might be confused, and your heart might be disappointed.

And that's okay. After all, a significant dating period virtually is a good indicator of whether a relationship can work, but it's still only a piece of the bigger picture.

Dating in person will be a very different experience, so really give yourself time and practice patience in order to allow the process to evolve. Note that this isn't a contradiction to my last point. I still believe that three dates will provide enough clarity if there's no potential; but if there is, both of you should acknowledge that there will be an adjustment period to match up the virtual version with the real-life version of each other. The exercise at the end of this chapter might help.

5. Apply the "Hands Off for Clarity" rule.

This is a hot dating topic that shocks singles when I bring it up.

I believe that it's ideal to refrain from touching while dating. Clarity within a relationship comes from connecting to what's in someone's brain and heart. You can gain that clarity a lot faster when you refrain from physical intimacy than you can otherwise!

In my previous book, *Get Real, Get Married,* I dedicated an entire chapter to this topic. Adding physical touch will confuse your brain and make the decision-making process much more challenging. For instance, you may like the physical intimacy and not be willing to break up even though you know this person is not your soulmate.

Basically, if there's no touch involved, how long would you really date someone you don't like? Not long at all, right? Which is exactly why this is an excellent tool for gaining clarity—and finding your husband or wife. As I mentioned previously, this is actually a big benefit of virtual dating. And because you've already got an initial connection going without physical touch, it makes even more sense to hold off and see whether this is a relationship that could really make it to marriage.

While I recommend not touching while dating, I recognize that some people choose to date in other ways. If you are one of those people, I highly recommend the Five Date Rule: don't touch for at least the first five dates. I know this can be particularly challenging, especially when you've already developed a connection online and this doesn't feel like your first five dates.... But consider what a powerful indicator of your potential it would be if you two get past those five dates with no touching and still want to continue dating.

6. When in doubt, go out.

You know that feeling of just not knowing whether you want to go out on a second date? Or even a sixth one? Like the dates are fine...but not much more than that? Or some go really well and some are downright boring? Like there's no good reason to keep going out...but there's also no good reason to call things off?

If so, you're in good company! Just about everybody finds themselves dating someone that they're just really not sure about at one point or another.

Now, in this case, you're not starting from ground zero because you've been virtually dating until this point, which may help you in getting that clarity. But it may just as easily confuse you even more because, as we mentioned in point #3, the person you're dating in real life is a fuller version of the one you dated online. You might need more time to figure out what, if anything, happens next.

In this case, I always tell clients, "Date 'em till you hate 'em."

Now, I know you're probably thinking, "But Aleeza, that wouldn't be fair! I don't want to lead anyone on." Don't worry, you're not leading anyone on. It's literally what dating is! People go out when they are unsure in order to find that clarity. You need to spend more time together and go through the dating process to decide if you two can make this work. The only way to have clarity is to gather more information. And the only way to get more information is to actually spend more time dating them.

So, if it's not a hard no, with reasons to back up that no, it's a yes for now. Put your effort in and make it work until it doesn't work. Then you'll know what to do. Give your brain and heart time to figure things out, and you will get your answer. And an answer that you'll never look back on and wonder about.

Takeaway: Both you and your date will likely be different when you meet in person from what you each imagined as you got to know each other virtually. Give yourself time and practice patience as you go through the transition process.

Exercise: Clear Your Confusion

After you meet your person in person, use the following space to help clear out your brain, understand what you're feeling and process it all. Jot down any conflicting realities between your virtual and in-person dating experiences (i.e. I saw/thought this about my date/our relationship, but really...).

_____

_____

_____

_____

_____

_____

_____

_____

Once you have it all written down, I highly recommend you share this with a mentor or dating coach to help you figure out what to do with this information.

Chapter Thirteen:
From "I Like You" to
"I Want to Marry You"

"There are no accidental meetings between souls."
– Sheila Burke

So you've been in a relationship for a significant amount of time already. You're feeling happy and hopeful. But there's one question still on your mind: is this partner the one?

What you're looking for and need in this moment is clarity.

You can take your first step toward clarity by looking at three components in your relationship: values, fears and irritants. Let's explore each of these a little bit.

Values

With your own values in mind, decide what values are most important to you in a partner. What top five to ten values does your partner need to embody in order for you to feel like this is a good match? Do not think about your current partner as you do this thought exercise. This is about YOU and what is most important to YOU in a partner.

Now, consider whether your current partner embodies those qualities. How strongly do they exhibit them? Use these questions to help you logically decide whether what you want and need in a relationship currently exists in your relationship.

Now, if you have a list of values, and your partner embodies most, but not all, of them, those that he or she doesn't embody become potential deal breakers. We'll address that shortly.

Fears

Again, without considering your current partner, think about what you are most afraid of in a relationship. Do you worry about infidelity or divorce? Are you concerned about codependency or health issues? You should have about three to five top fears that you might be bringing with you from childhood experiences or past relationships.

Now, compare how you typically feel about these fears versus how you feel about them with your current partner. Does he or she trigger these fears to a high degree, or actually help you feel more secure? Does your partner make you feel more concerned about your fears, or does he or she calm them?

If your partner lowers your feeling of fear, that's a good thing. If however, they actually trigger your fear, this could also be a potential dealbreaker.

Irritants

You also need to think about what irritates you about your partner. This time, I want you to think about your current partner specifically. Do they have habits or traits that frustrate you? Little quirks or qualities that kind of bother you or just drive you absolutely nuts?

Know that these are things that are not likely to change about them. You might feel that your partner will change their behavior or adapt to your preferences because they genuinely love you, but this is often not the case. (And it's not because they don't love you. It's just a natural trait or ingrained habit that isn't going anywhere.) I recommend that when you evaluate your partner, assume that their negative qualities will stay as they are. How open are you to accepting these qualities, habits or quirks? What can you tolerate, and what can you just not look past?

The more it bothers you and the less okay you are with tolerating it, the more of a dealbreaker it becomes.

So what do you do with all those potential dealbreakers?

When trying to get clarity within a relationship, I encourage my clients to focus on the potential dealbreakers rather than on the good parts. While, obviously, the more synchronicity there is—the more closeness in values, the fewer fears and irritants—the better off a couple is, all the positive aspects of a relationship won't keep it together if the negative is stronger than the positive. And sometimes, it takes only one or two negative aspects (which could be as simple as a highly rated value for one partner, such as religion, not being embodied by the other) to totally topple the relationship.

It's important to note that just because there are a few potential deal breakers, that does not mean that the relationship is doomed to fail. It does mean that they need to be addressed and sorted through before making any sort of long-term commitment. Ignoring them or pretending to accept them, but not actually doing the inner work necessary to actually accept them, will only come back to bite you later.

I want to note that a number of these issues are what I call "me issues" rather than "we issues." When you're in a relationship, it can be very easy to get caught up in the feeling that since you have a partner and you're both in the relationship, every problem that crops up needs to be addressed by both of you. But this is absolutely untrue. So many issues that come up in a relationship are about one partner, not both.

If you have a fear of divorce because your parents got divorced when you were young, or you simply can't stand people who bite their nails, those are "you issues." Your partner is not responsible for your childhood nor is it their problem that you think nail biting is gross. Your partner may or may not take a role in helping you work through these things, but don't expect them to, don't count on it, and know that, ultimately, it's your stuff to sort through.

Focus on your relationship, on figuring out whether there's long-term potential, on ensuring that you address the potential dealbreakers. When all is said and done, if you're ready to move forward, trust that this person is for you and make them your soulmate by marrying them.

Takeaway: Understanding the alignment between you and your date allows you to identify the next steps to take in your relationship.

Exercise: Dealbreaker Discussion

Keep this exercise handy for when you're in a relationship. Using the guidelines in this chapter, list 3 to 5 potential dealbreakers.

1._____

2._____

3._____

4 _____

5._____

Now, reflecting on those potential dealbreakers, take some time to consider whether those are "me issues" or "we issues." By being able to separate the two, and explore where these dealbreakers fall, you'll have clarity on what your next steps need to be—whether that's therapy, more time together in order to see how things play out, break up, get engaged, work on some internal stuff, have a conversation with your partner, etc.

1._____ Me/We Issue (circle)

   Now what? _____

   _____

2. _____ Me/We Issue (circle)

   Now what? _____

   _____

3. _____ Me/We Issue (circle)

   Now what? _____

   _____

4. _____ Me/We Issue (circle)

   Now what? _____

   _____

5. _____ Me/We Issue (circle)

   Now what? _____

   _____

VIRTUAL DATING

Conclusion

"If you own a smartphone, you're carrying a 24/7 singles bar in your pocket."
– Aziz Ansari

And...that's a wrap!

I hope that you have found this book helpful, that you now have the wisdom you need to handle virtual dating. I want you to feel confident in the belief that you can successfully date virtually, and that you have the inner strength to be patient through this process.

I know there's a lot of information here to process. I recommend reading through this book once and then going back to reread each section as it becomes relevant along your dating journey.

Before I sign off, I have one last evaluation exercise for you to complete. Similar to the first exercise you did, this is a self-assessment. I hope it helps you understand how you'd like to incorporate the ideas in this book into your dating experience.

Exercise: Virtual Dating Takeaways

Part 1: Rate your feelings

On a scale of 1 to 10, how do you feel about virtual dating as of this moment? (1 = Meh. Never really liked the idea of it and I'm pretty skeptical that it could actually work for me; 10 = I think it's an awesome way to date and am confident I can find my soulmate through virtual dating)

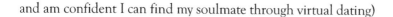

— 1 — 2 — 3 — 4 — 5 — 6 — 7 — 8 — 9 — **10** —

Most likely, this number has increased from the first time you did this assessment. If it didn't, don't worry. That means one of two things. Either you've discovered that virtual dating is really not for you—and that's a helpful discovery—or you're just feeling overwhelmed by all the information you've just absorbed. In the latter case, I suggest you come back in a few weeks to reassess.

Part 2: Own your tools

What new tools have you learned from this book? How will you implement these moving forward? (You don't have to have it all figured out right now, but putting a starting point down will help you actually take action and move forward.)

_____

_____

_____

_____

_____

Part 3: Identify your mentors

If you still feel like you are struggling through virtual dating, take some time now to think about who can help you navigate this journey. These can be mentors, friends, family members, or a dating coach. (We are always available to help! Visit marriagemindedmentor.com to read about our team and find the right coach for you.)

_____

_____

_____

_____

_____

Thank you for joining me on this virtual dating journey. I love hearing updates! Don't hesitate to be in touch and let us know about your dating successes: coach@marriagemindedmentor.com

May you gracefully navigate the virtual dating process, prepare to meet your soulmate, and find someone wonderful.

Blessings,

Aleeza Ben Shalom

Dedication

This book is dedicated in loving memory of my beloved friend, teacher and mentor, Rabbi Michael Stern of Rabbi Without Walls. He was a gifted relationship builder, and remains an inspiration for the dating coaching work I do today. Our friendship traversed many years and many states, and continued to grow and strengthen as, together with my husband, we explored and navigated a virtual relationship long before it was the norm. My husband, my family and I would not be where we are today if not for the warmth, love and guidance of Rabbi Mike. May his memory be a blessing.

Gratitude

To my beloved husband, Gershon, I love you so much. I feel blessed to be on our life journey together. As we are about to be celebrating 18 years together, I am reminded where we began and how you have always supported my work. Thank you for believing in me, loving me and encouraging me to do this work. I'm loving you!

To my loving children, Dovid Lev, Miriam, Moshe Chai, Yehuda Yosef and Avraham Levi, you are my sunshine! I love you so much, you make me so happy. Thank you for your patience as I was busy working to help others find love and build beautiful families like ours. May you each find your someone to love and treasure in the right time, and may it be with ease.

Dad, you have always helped me to think big and strive for more. No matter what I did, you encouraged me and inquired, "What's next?" Then you helped me plan it out and make my vision a reality. Thank you for always being my sounding board, for your support and business wisdom. I love you. Mom (of blessed memory) would be so happy to see us working on such great projects together.

To my beloved Mother-in-Law and Father-in-Law, thank you for spending time with the children as I was busy working. Your love and support has helped me to gradually and gracefully grow my business and help other couples to find what you have: a deeply meaningful relationship. Thank you for being amazing role models of a couple who has been married for nearly 60 years!

To my sister, Jessica Bird, I LOVE YOU SO MUCH! You mean the world to me. You have been my business mentor and loving support over the last few years. I can hear mom's wisdom through your voice and I love your guidance and how you nurture my creativity. Thank you for picking me up when I was down and for encouraging me to do more. I love you, sista!

Sara Zoldan, my soul sister. I love working with you. Without you there would be no book! May your endless hours and heroic efforts be rewarded not only in this lifetime but in the World to Come. You have helped me empower singles to manifest their soulmates. I love you and am so grateful we met. I'm even more grateful you joined my team! You are an incredible force in this world and I feel so blessed to work with you! I fully support you and your amazing work, and especially your unique mission to empower women to find love at any size. May we have many more years together helping singles find the One!

To my amazing team of information gatherers and behind-the-scenes support, thank you! Ira Somers and Carly Goldberg, you are dream makers. Without your support, this book may have just stayed a dream. Instead, thanks to your willingness to be the first to jump on board and help me get my ideas down on paper, it became a reality. Thank you and I love working with you!

To my incredible coaches Leah Cheirif, Regan Weiss, Ilana Brown, Shira Alt and Michael Dear, you have been so supportive along this journey. Thank you for transmitting these concepts to our clients. We have entered a new world of dating. Forevermore we will use these tools to help our clients make meaningful connections. I can't wait to hear about more client success stories and engagements. (For a free intro session with one of our coaches visit us at marriagemindedmentor.com)

To Alisa Brooks, my editor and personal writing mentor, I simply love working with you. We have been working together for a decade, infusing the world with more love. I can't wait for you to edit my next book! Thank you, I love your work! (You can find her online at alisabrookscoaching. com. Hire her! She's a pleasure to work with.)

To Joanna Dion Brown, my cover designer, interior layout expert and friend. Somehow I always have a rushed deadline and you tell me, "It's okay, we'll get it done." You're an angel. Thank you for working so efficiently! (If you need someone for a book cover or layout, you can reach Joanna at joannadionbrownart@gmail.com)

To my proofreaders, thank you! A book is good but a well edited book is great! No matter how many times a book is checked there will always be a mistake or a few when we go to print. Thanks to your efforts I hope there will be far fewer mistakes! Cheers to my proofreaders: Richard Aiken, Janinne Bracha Shor, Robert Goodman, Janis Fine, Meira Schnieder-Atik, Shoshi Glazer and so many others who have given feedback along the way.

To my beloved friends who told me the title and subtitle wasn't exactly right...thank you for being honest and helping me name and rename this book! What are we up to 5, 25 or 125? I don't know anymore! But thank goodness we hit the nail on the head finally. A special thank you goes out to Chana Mason and Adina Rubin. Get ready for my next book, I'm giving you notice I need your brain power and late night brainstorming sessions!

To Daniel Weiss, you've always been there to guide me in just the right way at just the right time. Thank you for saving me from myself! You're on my to call list and will be hearing from me often.

To my relatives, mentors and dear friends (you know who you are), I have learned so much from you. Thank you for supporting me and being there for me always.

To all my clients over the years, you are my inspiration. Your needs constantly guide my content. I will always do my best to deliver inspiration and support for your journey. Thank you for allowing me a place to share my wisdom. Your heartfelt emails and messages are what propel me forward! May you find your soulmate this year and make many happy memories together.

To the One Above, wow! What a journey You've taken me on. Thank You for blessing my every step and preparing me for what is to come. I feel blessed and grateful for the abundance You shower upon me and all of my clients.